EXERCISING YOUR DREAM

How to teach with passion,
express your purpose,
&
earn a living bringing happiness to others
in the boutique fitness industry

Ofelia de La Valette

Exercising Your Dream
How to teach with passion, express your purpose & earn a living bringing happiness to others in the boutique fitness industry

ISBN: 978-1727459401 (Paperback)
Front cover and book design by Paulina de La Valette
Edited by Roberta Nasci
Cover photo by Bubba Carr
Printed in the United States of America.
September 2018

Self-published by dance 101®
2480 Briarcliff Rd NE
Atlanta, GA, 30329
www.dance101.org

For Paulina and Erik

CONTENTS

My Invitation to You

Introduction: What Makes an Extraordinary Teacher   v

PART 1
THE JOURNEY BEGINS WITH US

PART 2
YOUR CLASS

PART 3
THE BUSINESS SIDE OF TEACHING

PART 4
SELF-CARE: TEACHING FOR THE LONG RUN

MY INVITATION TO YOU
Crossing the Line Requires a Leap of Faith

"The spirit calls, I must surrender."
- Lailah Gifty Akita

I never intended to write a book.

About a year ago, I conceptualized a teacher training course that would uniquely focus on every aspect of teaching except the actual content of the class (the material being taught). The course was intended for teachers in the boutique fitness industry who were already (or newly) certified to teach dance, dance fitness, barre, yoga, spinning, etc. but had not been trained in teaching methods, were unfamiliar with the inner workings of the industry and had limited understanding of how to create, deliver, market and manage a successful class over the long run. This course would expose all the "gotchas" that might blindside a newly minted teacher: delving into student expectations, studio politics, burnout, disastrous studio exits (that can sabotage a career), unexpected injuries, compensation, over committing to class load, and otherwise sharing wisdom that, until now, teachers had to learn by painful trial and error and over the course of many years.

The idea was a bit radical, as I could not find any teaching courses or workshops that addressed the subjects I would be covering, and as I set out to write the manual upon which the course would be built, something unexpected happened. What began as a training manual quickly crossed the line into something very different than what I had originally envisioned: a book! As words spilled from my mind and onto these pages hour after hour, day into night, weeks into months it became very clear to me that although my fingers were typing an instruction manual, a book was begging to be written. If you ask me, I am a teacher, not a writer. However, some greater force outside and within me busted through this self-imposed label and sat me down in front of a keyboard for hours on end.

I had no choice but to surrender to this process, on a leap of faith, that I was being guided in the direction I needed to go. The process of writing took a hold of me with a driving sense of purpose, holding me tightly in its grip for nine months in which I hermited myself, holed up in my home office, declining social invitations, occasionally forgetting to shower and disconnecting myself from the world outside of my office window. Were it not for the demands of running multiple studios, as well as teaching weekly classes, I would not have left my house while I wrote this book. My commitment to this work was indeed that powerful!

During this process, I began noticing how I was putting into practice the principles outlined in this book with every chapter I wrote—and this took me by surprise. I learned that the process of writing a book is strikingly similar to that of creating a class experience. Both require a driving sense of purpose that is impossible to ignore. Both require an organized delivery of content, the setting of objectives, preparation of the material being taught, implementation of teaching methods, and an opening and a close.

The parallels between writing this book and creating a class are so numerous I stopped pausing to reflect upon them and simply accepted that this dynamic would follow me all the way through to the end, which it did. Creation, by definition, is the action or process of bringing something into existence. Much like a class, or a business, this writing began with a singular thought: a desire to fill a need. Consider how this applies to any class you teach: Just like a class fills a need to facilitate a healthy lifestyle among those seeking one; this book fills a need to promote awareness among professional athletes who desire to create this experience for others. The creation of either begins with the desire to bring an experience into existence. Parallel number one . . . but there are others.

The parallel between creating a class and crafting a fulfilling and joyful life are similar as well. There have been plenty of moments in which I'd push my chair back from my desk questioning what this book was really about. Is this book about teaching movement or about the search for synchronicity between who we are by nature and

> **" I learned that the process of writing a book is strikingly similar to that of creating a class experience.**

the external world that encircles us? The answer of course is both—because when we work to craft an extraordinary class for others, we are in fact crafting an extraordinary life for ourselves. What we do in one area, spills over into another. That's the way it works. If you bring joy to others, how can you not experience the same joy? If your class strengthens another's body, how would your body escape the same benefit?

If we look at what is driving this process, the same principles apply across the board to anything we wish to create for ourselves or others. Case in point: Creation requires two catalysts and these are faith and courage; faith that we are fulfilling a greater purpose and the courage to respond to the driving force propelling us in that direction. Faith and courage are big, oftentimes scary words that require action that is usually outside, of our comfort zone. Faith requires us to embrace unsubstantiated safety and courage requires us to believe in ourselves. Both are strongly rooted in the acceptance that when a nagging desire grips us, it's the universe calling upon us to fulfill a particular karma. Choosing to put the paddle down as we are struggling against the current and allow that current to carry us in a different direction requires faith that we are safe in doing so. This is how I surrendered to the current and allowed my training manual to become this book and how you very well may have surrendered to any number of things in your life including your desire to teach. When we embark on a new path, we must believe the door has opened because we are meant to walk through. Had I fought against the current, you would not be holding this book nor reading these words.

Consider this metaphor as you contemplate answering a calling to enter into this profession or seeking to sharpen your existing teaching skills. Trust the process. If you find yourself on a slippery slope as you journey through Part 1 of this book, hang in there. If Part 2 overwhelms you with so much information, step back and take a breath.

> **Faith requires us to embrace unsubstantiated safety and courage requires us to believe in ourselves.**

Part 3 will give you great perspective on the industry and by the time you reach Part 4, you will have a deeper appreciation for the need to take care of yourself: mind, body and spirit.

As you stand on the threshold of creation, or at a crossroads in your teaching career, the best advice I can give you is to follow your heart. Believe in yourself and in the greater purpose your heart is nagging you to fulfill. Trust in the benevolence of the universe. Trust that you are being steered in the direction you need to go and surrender to this force. Commit to the journey. Embrace the adventure. Educate yourself. Grow. The rest will take care of itself.

Up until now, I have been on a solitary journey in writing this book. This is about to change because the moment you turn this page, you will come on board. Together we will travel through these chapters and process the enormous amount of information contained herein. I promise to make it fun when I can and to put things into perspective when I can't. The important thing for you to remember throughout these chapters . . . is the reason you picked up this book to begin with.

Warmly,

Ofelia

INTRODUCTION
What Makes an Extraordinary Teacher?

*D*early Beloved, we have gathered here today... I often find these words stuck in my head on a continuous loop when confronting the vagaries of life. It reminds me of how life (the noun) is the experience of living (the verb); each of us on our journeys separately, yet conjointly. We are in this life together, continuously "jumping" from one experience to another in a long succession of one thing after another, day in and day out, squeezing in as many moments of joy we can seize. Our lives can be such a quandary— often a series of "Why did this happen?", "What do I do about it?", "How do I handle this?", "Is this the right decision?" and "Why did I/he/she say that?" This is the "thing called life" and how gracefully we move through it, has much to do with the level of understanding and awareness we possess about ourselves and others.

What does any of this have to do with teaching movement? The answer is: EVERYTHING.

In your yoga, barre, dance, or Spinning class, on any given day, you will come face to face with a group of souls you likely may not intimately know. Each one represents a different sum of life experiences, each with his/her own values, filters, perspective, beliefs and personalities, each, like you, trying to make sense of life and the experiences thrown their way. And although these souls have come to your class for any number of reasons, they bring "themselves" with them.

> **A class is a gathering of souls, that come together for a shared experience which you are leading.**

Human beings are complex. While we are all moving through life together, we each bring a different perspective into the common experiences we share. A teacher's ability to hold space for others to be who they are has great bearing on whether the "gathering" is fulfilling beyond its singular purpose for being.

What brings students into your class often may not be the same reason they return. Their attendance may initially stem from a desire to benefit from your knowledge, to learn what you are willing to teach and/or to experience the class you've created. Each student will have their own set of expectations. Some may want to sweat, some may want to have fun, some may need a break from their obligations to others, some may be working towards certain fitness goals, others may want to learn something new and some may have a variety of expectations all bundled together. This may be what brings them in the first time, but, what motivates them to return has a lot to do with you.

Your success in meeting any of these, or other expectations of which you may not be aware, requires you to establish an outward connection to each person. It's this human connection that forms the basis of a relationship. Anyone who returns to your class is engaging in a relationship with you and others in the class. How do you foster the creation of these relationships?

Your ability to connect with a group of strangers requires you to be a neutral presence, to be receptive to incoming information and to respond with acceptance and warmth. The people present in your class were not chosen by you. You were chosen by them. Establishing relationships with people we choose is one thing. Establishing relationships with strangers who choose us is another. A successful class is built upon returning students. A returning student is a relationship. The curation of these types of relationships requires neutrality in our perspective and the only way I know how to achieve this begins with a deep understanding of ourselves.

The day we awaken to the realization that every soul is the life sum of their experiences, is the day a new door can open for us to have compassion towards others—if we choose. This requires an inner journey of self-discovery. Because once we understand ourselves, a space can exist in our hearts for others to be who they are. If we embrace acceptance, we empower ourselves to be a neutral force of nature. Extraordinary teachers hold no harsh judgment towards their students. They are conduits of love and acknowledgement.

❝ Your ability to connect with a group of strangers requires you to be a neutral presence, to be receptive to incoming information and to respond with acceptance and warmth.

The boutique fitness industry that you are in (or are entering) is a highly competitive market. With the proliferation of yoga, barre, Spinning and dance studios, your students have many choices. Gone are the days when only a few studios were spread across town. Students who appear in your class have done so specifically for the experience you offer and let me tell you, they are demanding. Twenty plus years in the dance industry has taught me that students are looking for four things from every movement class they take:

- They want to have fun and be among friends
- They want to sweat
- They want to accomplish goals
- They want to be seen.

By "seen" I mean they don't want to be invisible, they want to be acknowledged for their presence. An exceptional class delivers on all four, which is no small feat. This requires much more than simply knowing your content and showing up. You must create a connection with each student, be accepting, be interested, kind, open and deliver the physical experience they are seeking.

You are holding this book and reading these words because you are curious about what it takes to be exceptional in this line of work. You may be surprised to learn that the journey to excellence begins within. Or maybe you already knew that. Either way, the journey undeniably begins with us . . . and that is what Part 1 of this book is about.

What makes an extraordinary teacher?

Outstanding credentials are only one piece of the equation. While some teachers will use their degrees, certificates, and experience to justify their credentials, I must say that throughout my career as a dance studio owner and a dance teacher, I have observed how that does not make them automatically "exceptional" teachers. Credentials are one side of the coin and, although surely significant, alone are not enough to inspire an entire class, to maximize the potential of each student or to reshape bodies and touch hearts.

Consider the following:

1. Great teachers have clarity

- They know how to clear themselves of preconceived prejudices —this facilitates the acceptance of others.
- They are able to block judgment based upon assumptions—this can interfere with the perception of other's motives.
- They are able to distinguish between useful and destructive feedback—this increases the efficacy of their delivery.

2. Great teachers have the ability to "see" students from a neutral, humane, and compassionate perspective.

No one is invisible in their classroom. These teachers connect, empathize, inspire, and motivate. A critical step in the process of becoming a great teacher is recognizing one's personal approach to the world. By understanding ourselves, we are able to become aware of the "window" through which we see, perceive, and respond to others. This knowledge can also help us to be more accepting of others who, like us, are most likely being "held captive" by personality traits and learned behaviors which may or may not be conscious.

3. Great teachers do not project any self-limiting beliefs onto their students! They simply hold space for their students to be who they are. They accept their students in that moment of their journey without misjudging them, making them feel inadequate or trying to manipulate any outcome. They are compassionate, offer unconditional support, and always provide the right amount of information as it is needed. In their classroom, these teachers work within self-established parameters

for learning. These parameters can embrace certain teaching strategies such as encouraging students to maintain an open mind, to test their limits, have faith in their abilities, and to understand that the body learns through practice.

4. **Great teachers understand that they are in service to their students.** They are receptive to their students' needs and welcome their recommendations with a positive attitude. What might otherwise be regarded as complaints and criticism are recast as "feedback" and "suggestions". Great teachers make the distinction between who they are and what they do. Because of this, they are not insulted by constructive feedback. These teachers approach the evolutionary path of their teaching with the understanding that growth is only made possible by way of new information. They know that in the absence of external feedback, there is only stagnation. The world around us is constantly shifting in new directions and the only way to stay in step with it is by being receptive to change. Teachers whose classes evolve concurrently with shifting demographics, trends, culture and suggestions for improvement are the ones who thrive over the long term.

5. **Great teachers are protective of their students' class experience.** They take care to create and maintain the best possible environment for learning. And while pleasing everybody is an unrealistic objective, consideration for the whole of the class is greatly appreciated by the many who are present. From the smallest of details like the air temperature and the cleanliness of the studio floor to the more intrusive occurrences like someone talking on their phone during class or a student invading another's space or talking over the teacher and being disruptive require a teacher to be in command and

control by demonstrating leadership. Again, we are all in this together. The unruly behavior of one will affect the many and students will look to the teacher to protect their class experience. Great teachers understand this and respond accordingly (but always with tact, compassion and warmth!).

6. **Great teachers know their stuff.** Although this is a given and shouldn't require an explanation, it should appear on this list. The only thing I would add here is that while extraordinary teachers are constantly working on their craft and are current on any advancements in their chosen speciality, they don't pretend to have all the answers. While their knowledge is extensive, one can't know everything. If a student asks a question that stumps a teacher, the great ones will respond honestly with: "I don't know the answer to that, but I will find out and get back to you, is that ok?" Making up an answer in order to avoid the awkwardness of not knowing is never the right path. Great teachers are confident in themselves and they are magnanimous.

7. **Great teachers conduct themselves with utmost professionalism.** They have tremendous respect for their students and for their studio. Whatever may be going on in their lives, they check their "suitcase" at the door, "neutralize" themselves and enter with a smile. They do not speak negatively to students about other students or the studio. They express concern for student grievances, remain impartial and bring the grievance to the attention of management. They do not throw another log onto the fire, joining in on the complaint or spreading gossip. They also don't burden their students with their problems or vent about a dispute they may be having with studio management. Professionalism in the classroom also helps to ensure a seamless class experience. Students should not be

burdened by that which does not involve them. Everybody is dealing with a multitude of things in their lives already. Great teachers keep their classes light and carefree as much as possible.

8. **Great teachers practice gratitude.** Teaching movement is a wonderful profession. Not everyone is suited for it and the ones who are, are truly blessed. Great teachers appreciate this blessing and their expression of gratitude is contagious. As author Lynne Twist, so famously said: *"What we appreciate, appreciates"*. She has also been quoted as saying *"We are not grateful because we are happy, we are happy because we are grateful"*. Gratitude acts like a magnet. Its field of energy radiates far from its source. A classroom is an enclosed space that contains and holds energy. Gratitude is so powerful, it can blanket a room. Everyone in its periphery can be tagged by it. Teachers who show up with gratitude for their class and everyone in it create a loving atmosphere that is a joy for others to be in.

9. **Great teachers are awesome DJs.** The music they play in their classes elevates their class experience to even greater heights. They regularly update their playlists with thoughtful consideration for each song. Mining for great music is a weekly habit. Great teachers understand that movement must be repetitive in order for students to master them. These teachers will use music to entertain and to alter the experience of the material they are teaching (even if slightly), keeping their students engaged, interested and inspired. The music they play in class is the finishing touch.

This book is not just about teaching. It's about exceptional teaching and as with anything exceptional, a deeper dive into every relevant detail is necessary. We must take a look at ourselves, we must deliver an excellent class, we must understand the business we are in and we must conduct ourselves professionally. That's a lot of "musts". But this is what it takes to cross the line from good to great to exceptional.

PART 1
The Journey Begins with Us

One

"Life is 10% what you make it
and 90% how you take it."
- Irving Berlin

Our Blueprint Characteristics

*M*y stepfather is a behavioral psychologist and scientist who dedicated his career to the research of human behavior. He came into my life when I was eleven years old and three years later, my sister Isabel was born. Forty years ago, my stepfather would cringe if he were to read this chapter. If you are familiar with the work of B.F. Skinner *Beyond Freedom & Dignity (Penguin Books, LTD, 1971)*, you may recall his concept of "behavior modification" which is the belief that behavior is cast through the use of positive and negative reinforcement. My stepfather was a big fan of B.F. Skinner's theories and believed we are all shaped solely by our environment and that we are born with no preferences, no personality, no identity: a clean slate, essentially. He would not agree with any theory that proposed any element of "behavorial genetics" (although much has been published about this theory since the late 19th century). His strategy for raising my sister during her early formative years was with the use of M&M candy to reward desirable behavior (positive reinforcement). The rule was: one piece of candy per desired behavior. This strategy made sense to me at the time and my mother, brother and I all participated as instructed, with a large bag of M&Ms always on the ready.

I grew up believing my stepfather was somewhat of a genius. A Cuban immigrant, he earned his Ph.D. at Harvard University and went on to publish numerous papers in scientific journals. My mother used to call him the "absent minded professor". I chuckle when I remember the time she sent him out for groceries and he drove to his office and sat at his desk trying to remember why he was there. He returned home an hour later without any groceries and my mother sent him back out but this time with written instructions (one of my fondest memories of him)! I credit my stepfather for piquing my interest in psychology. In high school I would read his textbooks (the case histories were of particular interest to me) and for a time I thought about majoring in psychology. Life had other plans for me, but throughout my life I've maintained a fascination with the science of the mind.

What you will read in the following pages and chapters is not scientific. Although much of my thoughts about behavior have a basis in empirical data I have accumulated over the course of my life, much of what is contained herein is anecdotal and originates from a spiritual perspective as well. Terms like "blueprint characteristics", "reactionary reflexes" and "assumptive judgment" are my own and many of the theories you are about to read have been influenced by my personal journey through life. This work is largely biographical and includes personal experiences and observations I've made over time. My hope is that you take what resonates with you and discard what doesn't. If this work hits a chord, brings you an "A-Ha!", or causes you to release a painful memory, I will feel my efforts to bring this awareness to you have been worthwhile.

So, get comfortable, open your mind and consider the following:

I believe our personalities spring from three fundamental wells of programming:

- Our blueprint characteristics (what we were born with)
- Our values and filters (the result of environmental conditioning)
- Our self-image (how we have learned to see ourselves through others)

In this chapter we will discover how our blueprint characteristics form the foundation of our personalities. These are the characteristics or tendencies we were born with.

Detecting blueprint characteristics is easiest with children from birth to four years because they have not yet fully developed a conscious awareness. They are in their purest form of being, absent of any filters, values, and self-image. These evolutionary aspects of our personality come later in life and continue to evolve over time. Our blueprint; however, is constant. It's the unshakable underpinning upon which all aspects of our learned behavior rests.

The blueprint's job is to preserve itself while maintaining and protecting its original characteristics. Our automatic reactionary tendencies, a.k.a. all those wonderful "knee-jerk" reactions we all love about ourselves (just kidding), are the consequent mechanisms that protect the blueprint. The first thing we want to look at in our journey towards self-awareness is to identify what situations trigger which certain reactions in us. This helps us to put these unconscious reflexes or behavioral habits into proper context.

The easiest way to do this is to recall to memory unfamiliar situations we were exposed to for the first time and to remember how we naturally reacted in those situations. Some situations might have been difficult and to recall them might feel painful. The key here is to gently allow oneself to re-feel those dormant feelings. Writing them down will help us release them from our sub-conscious mind (instead of carrying them around with us and into our relationship dynamic) and will help our mind and body to relax. This mindful practice will help us reveal very insightful information about ourselves and the blueprint we were born with.

> **Our blueprint; however, is constant. It's the unshakable underpinning upon which all aspects of our learned behavior rests.**

For a more practical understanding, here's my story:

It was a fateful day in October 1960 when my brother, then 5 years old and I, 3 years old, each took my mother's hand and boarded a ferry from Havana to Key West. My father had flown out of Havana a few weeks prior on what ended up being one of the last commercial flights to JFK Airport in New York. Having left Cuba ahead of us to prepare for our arrival, my father miscalculated the exodus of exiles as the public became increasingly fearful that flights to the U.S. would be canceled in the following months. Fidel Castro had risen to power earlier that same year and my father (who knew Castro from their time at the University of Havana) had a close eye on the Cuban government and the transition from capitalism to communism that was happening in sporadic bursts. Relations between the US and Cuba were deteriorating rapidly, people were fleeing the island and all available passenger seats were booked on the few remaining flights. Our only option was to leave by sea.

Down on the ferry dock, I remember sitting on my grandmother's lap and not understanding why she was crying.

With no idea that a decade would pass before I saw her again, I bounced up and down on her lap with excitement about riding in a huge boat! An adventure! We set off and I remember the boat being very crowded. Under my mother's watchful eye, I exhausted myself running in circles around the deck and making friends with the other children on the ferry boat. My brother sat quietly next to my mother. Approximately ten hours later we arrived in Key West. It was nightfall.

Over the years that ensued, my mother would re-tell the story of our journey from Havana to New York . . . much of what I write here belongs to her. I share it with you now through her memory of it as well as through the bits and pieces that were forever "etched" in my memory.

We disembarked from the ferry hungry and tired. Each of us carrying a small suitcase holding only what we were able to carry—which in my case, for a 3-year-old, was not a lot. My smart little leather suitcase with brass latches had my initials engraved upon it, with a name tag attached to the handle: My name, my address in Guanavacoa (a small town outside of Havana where we lived) and a phone number were written on it. On the back of the tag, my mother wrote a note stating that if a little girl were found with this suitcase, the little girl belonged to her. In retrospect, I'm not sure how any of this information could have been helpful had we gotten separated. Rather, I think it only made my mother feel better to think someone, somehow would return me to her in the event we were separated. Although, truth be told, that would not have been likely. She held onto our hands so tightly it hurt, and as the story goes, I whined and complained about it the entire ride to the motel in Key West.

The motel was in the middle of nowhere, located on a winding two lane road with nothing for miles. The taxi sped off upon our exit from the backseat and my mother was left standing in front of the "reception desk", under a flashing neon Motel sign that illuminated her beautiful face. Darkness was falling all around us, it was late and the sound of the frogs and crickets in the heavy humid air seized my mother in a moment of realization of how far she was from home, completely alone and on her own. She was twenty-four.

She greeted the man at the reception desk in her limited, but elegant English and he showed us to our room. We dropped our suitcases and under protest (mainly from me), my mother dragged my brother and me to the bathroom for what was one of the most painful and thorough face, hand, and arm scrubbings I can remember. Joyous not to have lost any skin, I began jumping up and down on the mattresses and from bed to bed before loudly announcing that I was hungry.

There was no room service (as my mother had hoped) and no restaurant on the premises. The man at the reception desk directed my mother to the nearest establishment that offered food at that late hour—which (in retrospect) turned out to be a trucker bar about a mile down the road. With no taxi service available and in her elegant dress pumps, determined to feed her children, we set out on foot for the "restaurant" in pitch black night.

As the bar came into view, my mother became increasingly uncomfortable about entering the building. Trailer trucks and truck cabs were parked all around with a few cars here and there. Unsure of what she was walking into, she squeezed our hands more tightly as we made our way into the bar. You have to know at this point that my mother was a strikingly beautiful woman. Slender and elegant in her linen dress with her Elizabeth Taylor haircut, she had been a model for Christian Dior in Cuba prior to her engagement to my father. Every head turned as we entered the dimly lit bar. What a sight she must have been with her two little well dressed children in each hand.

We found a small table off to the side and my mother ordered an American hamburger, fries, and milk for us. A quick survey of the room mortified her. I was delighted.

My excitement was beyond containable and I struggled to remain in my seat. My eyes couldn't have been wider as I took it all in, particularly fascinated by the neon signs and flashing lights. There was loud music blasting from a nearby jukebox in a language I didn't understand. Repeatedly I jumped out of my chair to dance around the table. My brother sat frozen like a statue as my mother closed her eyes in disbelief over where we were, on that lonely road, at midnight, at that moment of time in her life.

With no taxi service available and in her elegant dress pumps, determined to feed her children, we set out on foot for the "restaurant" in pitch black night.

The story continues from this point on, containing many twists and turns as life does. But let's reflect and take a moment to observe what the story reveals about each of the character's blueprint (including mine). Through the narration of the story we can detect how each of us reacted differently to the same situation. By paying attention to these natural behavioral responses we can peek into the blueprint of my mother, my brother, and me, to identify what situations triggered which reactions and revealing the unconscious reflexes of behavior applied by each one to manage the situation. For example, my mother's character blueprint can be summarized as, fearful and courageous. My brother's, withdrawn and passive; and mine, curious and naive. Each of our blueprints contains many more characteristics, but these are a few of the more obvious ones revealed in this story. Please note: When describing a blueprint the adjectives used should not be labeled "good" or "bad" as each blueprint contains both capacities (curious and naive has gotten me into many a pickle whereas withdrawn and passive kept my brother out of a lot of trouble when we were kids!). What's important is the conscious knowledge we gain from our observation. The information about what is.

Let me complete this exercise by writing a short summary about how I perceive some of the characteristics of my own blueprint: I am curious. I trust that I'm safe to explore. I engage, connect, and interact. I am impatient and I have expectations about the outcome. I approach life as an adventure and I complain loudly when I'm being held back. My excitement takes over and I often miss the details. I tend to jump without looking, figuring out my landing as I'm falling.

Having the awareness of this knowledge about myself, I am better able to anticipate my natural reactions when I am placed in an unfamiliar situation (which is relatively frequent).

Now it's your turn; you can uncover a few (or many) of your own blueprint characteristics with this exercise. You will need a pen and a piece of paper or your journal. Draw three columns and label them: column A, column B, column C.

Ask a family member to help you recall a big event in your young life, for example: your first day of school, a trip, moving, or any other significant event. Allow his/her recollection to help you remember how you felt. Ask your family member to use adjectives to describe your behavior and write them under column A. In column B, list adjectives that describe how you felt. Some memories might feel painful; in this case, breathe gently and continue to proceed to fully feel that situation you are being guided to review. Write any feelings that arise in column B. The writing will help you release the tension of the memory. Once column A and column B are complete, take a look at the words in both columns and draw a line to connect adjectives in column A with those in column B that "speak to each other", or somehow belong together. Take your time; do not rush through this exercise. Think about and process what you are uncovering. Write your observations under column

C in the form of simple words, sentences or paragraphs. Once the big picture comes into focus, try to recognize what you see and feel without judgment or explanation. Try to absorb the "deeper truth" about yourself by acknowledging what is. This can be a magical moment in which your mind and heart expands to allow the revelation of the blueprint to show itself to you.

Being aware of your blueprint is the key to understanding how you are predisposed to react to your environment.

> **You and I must be aware of what we bring with us into a class. We must also be aware that what we bring belongs only to us. Our blueprint is what's packed inside our smart little leather suitcase with brass buckles and our name written on the tag.**

Every soul in your class will also arrive with a little suitcase. Imagine this when you walk into your class: Picture everyone present holding a suitcase. Believe me, this is a visual that packs a punch. It really does enhance the importance of self-reflection for anyone who hopes to exist cohesively among others, and even more so for anyone whose role is that of a teacher.

The realization that each and every one of us carries a blueprint through life (that we cannot alter) should be an eye-opener at the very least. Conversely, at its very best, this is a powerful enough "A-Ha!" to cause anyone to be more compassionate, forgiving, and accepting of others. Don't get me wrong, there are plenty of people in the world who are cruel, maybe even to you. However, if we are reminded of the suitcase, we can strive not to take their aggression personally. It's their luggage. We only stepped into the line of fire. Accept, forgive, and turn on your music. You have a class to teach.

> **" It really is very freeing to let go of any expectation or responsibility about what you don't understand is happening.**

Here's the thing: Once we realize and uncover our individual character blueprint, it becomes much easier to accept the blueprints of other people. I didn't design my blueprint; it came along with me as did yours—as everyone else's did. The most we can hope for is to do the best with what we're given and through the awareness of it, make accommodations when possible.

My blueprint of curiosity and trustfulness used to repeatedly put me in situations where I failed to see the danger around me—and still does occasionally when I'm not paying attention. I've been gullible and careless more than a few times in my life which has led me down paths I would have otherwise preferred to have avoided. Alternately, I've traveled paths which have delighted me. The key, again, is awareness of our tendencies.

This knowledge is powerful, and with time and practice it may become easier to let go of superficial judgment of others. Your teaching will benefit immensely from this. It really is very freeing to let go of any expectation or responsibility about what you don't understand is happening. Surrendering to this knowledge creates a space for acceptance to emerge.

Two

"Everything you think about yourself,
is because you learned it."
–Don Miguel Ruiz

Deconstructing Ourselves:
Values and Filters

*A*long with our blueprint, our little suitcase carries our values and filters. Our values are the byproduct of learned behaviors and are the force behind our actions. Our filters are the way we perceive and react to our reality based on the result of past experiences. We are not born with either of these; they attach themselves to us, influencing our behavior, as we go through life.

Filters

Filters are the lenses through which we process and react to information and account for much of the "why" we do what we do. We begin collecting filters during our infancy; however, until we develop conscious memory, they are stored in our subconscious mind. Our diaper is wet, we cry, our diaper is changed. Even the simplest instances of cause and effect establish filters in us which begin forming at birth. If you've ever wondered about a certain behavioral pattern of yours (how your filter perceives a situation and, therefore your reaction) that you can't really explain, chances are you acquired this filter in your subconscious as a result of a forgotten cause and effect.

Our filters determine how we perceive and react to life. When my mother was a very young girl of about 4 years old, she was having a picnic with her mother in the back yard of their house when, out of nowhere, a bullfrog jumped onto her lap. It so startled her she became frightened. If you hear my mother tell the story, that bullfrog weighed 50 lb and was the size of her lap (that much I do believe). From that day forward, my mother developed a lifelong fear of frogs. She did not understand this fear until one day she happened to mention it to her mother, who then told her the story about the picnic. My mother had not retained the memory in her conscious mind, but the filter had formed nonetheless.

As we grow older, it becomes a bit easier to explain how we acquire certain filters, if we are willing to take a closer look. When I was a freshman at the Universidad Complutense de Madrid in Spain, my godmother lived just outside the city in what I would describe as the most exquisite apartment I had ever seen. I remember the first time I walked into her foyer, freshly off an exhausting eight-hour charter flight from New York to Madrid. I was captivated. I experienced a very pleasant visceral reaction to the beauty before me which etched upon me an indelible mark. Meticulously clean, tidy, beautifully decorated in neutral colors and textures with stunning original art work—that apartment beckoned me to come in and relax. To this day, I make my bed and tidy up my home every morning before I leave for the day just so when I return I can experience that same feeling—and I do!

Uncovering our filters can take a lot of inner probing. While some are on the surface of our preferences and easier to detect, most lie in varying depths within us. I have found that the easy to identify filters are the most innocuous ones (because we know they are there). Uncovering these are a matter of taking a sweeping inventory of the life you've created for yourself and evaluating the varying ways you react to the behavior of others. The deeper

> " **Our filters determine how we perceive and react to life.**

filters like fear of frogs or early morning compulsive cleaning may require the assistance of a professional. But, before you call your "shrink in Beverly Hills", read on. There's more . . .

Values

Our values are imprinted upon us initially by our parents and later by extended family, community, and cultural influences. Whereas our filters are demonstrated through behavior (words + actions), our values are revealed via our beliefs. They are our moral and ethical compass, driven largely by how we were taught to regard and treat ourselves and others.

I was fortunate to have been given a good value system by my parents, especially by my mother. She was a somewhat disenfranchised woman until her later years when she was able to gain control of her circumstances. She achieved amazing things in her life, mostly toward the end, but while she was parenting my brother, sister, and me, she was a warrior. Life had dealt her some hard blows, uprooting her from her birth country, separating her from her family and friends and thrusting her into a foreign world she was unprepared to navigate. She struggled with these changes.

Nonetheless, she managed to instill in us strong values

such as kindness, compassion, and loyalty. She also encouraged us to chase our dreams, to believe in ourselves, specifically in regard to my sister and me, to fight for our rights, work very hard, find our voice, and not allow ourselves to be suppressed. My mother was a card carrying member of the National Organization of Women and Gloria Steinem was her hero. She wanted her girls to be confident, strong, and brave—values she was struggling to apply to herself. I often joke about how my mother enrolled my younger sister in karate when most of my sister's friends were taking ballet.

"As teachers, we must be aware of what we are carrying and endeavor to bring only the most relevant and useful aspects of our personalities into the classroom.

Over the years, I've been able to let go of some limiting values instilled in me by my mother, which had to do with scarcity and distrust, in favor of other more positive ones. And while I received self-defining values from my mother, it was my father who drilled work ethic into me—a value I've chosen to keep. I can still hear his voice inside my head instructing me to do everything and anything to the very best of my ability. No matter the task or the job, I was to give it 100 percent. Anything less was simply put, unacceptable.

It is important to uncover our blueprint and examine our values and filters because we bring them with us into every situation we encounter, including, but not limited to, every class we teach. As the saying goes, "wherever you go, there you are". As teachers, we must be aware of what we are carrying and endeavor to bring only the most relevant and useful aspects of our personalities into the classroom. If we have unexamined values, we carry the risk of imposing them upon others. This is something we should strive not to do. It may not be fair to the other person and worse, it may cause us to make an error in judgment about that person, which may cause us (and them) anguish.

Here's an example which illustrates the consequences of imposing self-values onto others. When I would see students in class "relaxing" instead of working, or not fully attempting to execute the movement I was teaching, it used to really bother me. I'd think to myself: "Why did they bother coming to class?" Sometimes it would irritate me so much, I'd allow it to break my concentration. Instead of focusing on what I was doing, I would focus on what they weren't doing and it would send me into a spiral. Then I met Ms. Lucy.

Ms. Lucy was, my best guess, in her late eighties possibly early nineties, when she first registered to take hip hop classes at dance 101. She was a tiny sliver of a thing; her body was frail, with extremely limited ability for movement. Walking was difficult for her. She moved very, very slowly. Someone would drive her to the studio, drop her off, and return an hour later to get her. She didn't speak much and her hand shook as she'd write her name on the sign-in sheet at the front desk. Ms. Lucy took virtually every hip hop class we had on the schedule at the time, with no concern about its level, beginner and advanced classes alike. It really didn't matter. In spite of what was going on around her, Ms. Lucy would stand in the back of the class and for an hour, she'd walk in place. I don't recall the last time Ms. Lucy took a class. I only remember my realization one day that I had not seen her in a while.

I never got a chance to thank Ms. Lucy for coming to the studio—much less for the lesson she unwittingly taught me. Sometimes it takes something really obvious on someone's outside for us to notice something that's not so obvious within us. It was a paradigm shift for me. Ms. Lucy just wanted to be at the studio, to be in a dance class, in a vibrant and youthful environment. She didn't really understand the music, or the song lyrics (thank goodness) but she heard the beat and felt the energy around her.

With Ms. Lucy, her limitations were on the surface, but with most people, they are hidden from view, as is their motivation for being in your class. During the course of your teaching career, you may encounter many "Ms. Lucys". These are people whose reasons for being in your class may not be what you assume them to be, and unless you are aware of your own values and filters, you may misjudge them. We cannot expect others to approach their lives in the same way we do. We should not impose our values on those around us. This is why it is so important to be aware that we have them and what they are, so we know when to set them aside.

Filters and Values

Filters (perception) come from values (internal moral and ethical compass/beliefs), and values reinforce filters. Filters and values are infinitely connected in a self-perpetuating circle. A child, who is treated kindly, is kind to others and treats others accordingly, who in turn may return the kindness to the child; therefore, reinforcing the kindness, and so, completing the circle.

This is the *behavior/value reinforcement dynamic*:

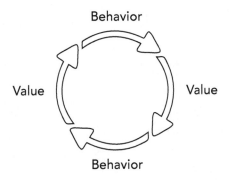

But, there is something else. Whereas our blueprint characteristics remain constant throughout our lives, values and filters can change. These changes occur when we typically allow new information to enter into our awareness. Ms. Lucy's example shows how we can be influenced by another person's story or set of circumstances. Or we may read a book, an article or watch a documentary that activates in us a process of reevaluation of our beliefs about a particular subject.

> **"eliminating behaviors without altering the value or belief system behind those behaviors will most likely result in only a temporary change. To modify our behavior successfully, we must address the values behind it.**

Or we may have an experience that leaves us with an indelible mark which may radically change certain values we had been holding. These are the catalysts that can cause a natural, organic change in our values, which in turn influences new behaviors.

For example: I continue to hold onto my value of giving 100 percent to everything I do. But since I realized that I cannot possibly know anyone's hidden motivation for doing anything, I've come to accept that all students in my class are doing the best they can pursuant to why they are there. This realization "rewrote" my value to read: "Everyone is giving his/her 100 percent including me". This is a new value that I have added to my collection.

Another catalyst for change may come from within ourselves. We may have recognized a certain pattern of repetitive behavior we engage in that consistently produces an outcome we'd prefer to avoid. However, eliminating behaviors without altering the value or belief system behind those behaviors will most likely result in only a temporary change. To modify our behavior successfully, we must address the values behind it.

This is the *behavior/value revision dynamic* and looks like this:

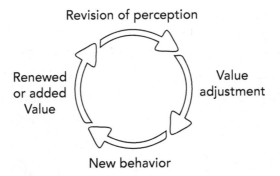

Revision of perception

Renewed
or added
Value

Value
adjustment

New behavior

The *behavior/value revision dynamic* is constantly at play, whether we realize it or not. It is the formula for change. Bottom line, if we wish to change something about ourselves, we must change how we think about that particular thing. How we perceive something dictates how we will react to it and how we react to something influences how we perceive it. It's an on-going circle of influence.

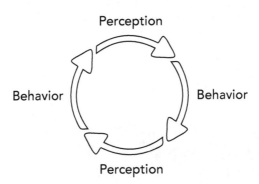

Perception

Behavior

Behavior

Perception

About a year ago, I changed my values surrounding food and became a Vegan. I am often asked if it was hard to make this change. Truth is, it wasn't difficult at all, because instead of focusing on changing my behavior, I focused on my reasons (values) for becoming vegan. Once a closely held value or belief changes, the behavior around it organically changes, with surprisingly little effort. As time passed, the absence of meat and dairy in my diet diminished my desire for it. The less I desired it and the better I felt physically, the more my value around it became stronger, perpetuating the circle of revision. The continuity of the behavior went on to reinforce my new belief about eating animal products. Had I simply stopped eating these foods without revising my value around it, I doubt I could have sustained it in the long run. At some point I would have said: "Forget this! Gimme a hamburger! What can it hurt?" And off the wagon I go.

As we prepare our mindset for teaching, we can use this awareness to make inner adjustments where needed.

The intention of this training is not to change you; rather, my purpose is to help guide you to a higher level of conscious understanding about the personal nature of perception. This knowledge can compliment or hinder the creation and delivery of your classes. These are important steps on the journey to exceptional teaching.

Three

"When life hands you limes, make mojitos."
–Sara J. Gonzalez (my mother)

Self-Image

Our blueprint characteristics and filters are largely behavioral. Our values espouse our beliefs. The question at this point is: "What do we think about it and how do we perceive it?" To answer this we should consider the binding element that tempers every aspect of how we present ourselves to the world—our self-image.

Picture a glass of ice water. Your blueprint is the glass, your values and filters are the ice, and the water that fills the glass is your self-image.

Our early stage self-image is largely defined by labels imposed upon us by individuals in our immediate circle of influence. These individuals include our parents, siblings, extended family, teachers, close friends, peers and other adults representing authority, safety and security in our lives. By the time we reach adolescence we may begin to challenge some of these labels. As we mature, we journey through a process of re-authoring these self-beliefs, consequently revising our self-image. Hopefully, at some point in our adulthood we will have cleared out as many self-damaging labels as possible and replaced them with new ones which champion our uniqueness and inner beauty. Our present day self-image may be a combination of both imposed and self authored beliefs.

Our self-image has great influence on every aspect of our lives. What we believe about ourselves dictates virtually every decision we make: Where we work, what we do, who we choose as a partner, friends we attract . . . everything. Because of this, the picture we hold of ourselves is the basis of understanding the life we've created for ourselves. It is also the first revision we must make if we wish to alter our future. As a teacher, our self-image enters into our class with us. How we regard ourselves has great influence on how we regard others. If we hold ourselves in a small place, we may hold others there too and vice a versa. For this reason, as teachers, we should take a look at the labels that make up the bricks and mortar of our personality.

> **The words you use to describe yourself are your inner mantras.**

Take a moment to grab a pen and paper. Number the page 1–30 and make a list of adjectives that describe yourself—whether or not you authored them—as these self defining adjectives describe your inner truth. Next, organize the content of your list into three categories. Highlight those you wish to keep, circle those you wish to improve and cross through those you wish to remove.

What did you notice about your list? What conclusions can you draw from the number of things you wish to improve or remove? How many connections can you make between your blueprint characteristics, your values and filters, and this list? Study these words and after you've given yourself time to reflect upon them, I want you to imagine you were to step outside of yourself as if you were a separate person observing yourself. Then write a few paragraphs describing what you have observed—i.e., your own perception of yourself.

Begin your first paragraph this way: "Allow me to introduce (insert your name here). He/She is . . . ." At this point let your description flow. The purpose of this exercise is not to figure out how the world perceives (or should perceive) you. Not everyone will see us as we see ourselves because people look through their own filters (that we are not responsible for). The purpose of this exercise is self-discovery. How do you see yourself?

The conclusions you draw from looking at yourself through your self-image may be quite revealing. The words you use to describe yourself are your inner mantras. You may not be aware of this, but all the words you just wrote down are constantly being verbalized in your psyche. I believe this is how we communicate our expectations to the universe. The Law of Attraction supports this. What we attract in our lives is related to how we see and think about ourselves. If we wish to attract something different, we must redefine ourselves accordingly. If we want success, our self-image must be that of a successful person, even though there is no environmental evidence to substantiate our success in that very moment. People who think of themselves as successful will achieve success. No loser ever achieved success. In fact, a winner is a loser who tried one more time. What keeps the loser trying? A healthy self-image of being successful.

Look at your list again and re-read your introduction. Is it complete? Does it contain all that you wish to manifest for yourself? If not, take extra time to add in what's missing!

Four

"When we respect everybody around us, we are in peace
with everybody around us."
– Don Miguel Ruiz

Reactionary Reflexes

N ow that we've taken a look at ourselves, let's examine how we react to our surroundings.

During the course of your teaching career you will meet many different people. Unexpected things may be said and it can happen during a class.

Recognizing how we react to certain situations is an important step in the process of becoming a successful teacher. By understanding our own approach to life, not only can we improve how we respond to others, but we also know when to subtract our prejudices and preferences from a situation to let it reveal itself for what it really is.

Each one of us has values surrounding how we wish to be treated, spoken to, and regarded. Further, many of us impose onto others the values by which we govern ourselves. We have opinions about how people should behave around us or in general. Oftentimes we make assumptions about why people are expressing themselves in a certain way. We may issue judgment upon those who do not share our values, or have values we disagree with. These are natural tendencies we all have to some extent and an exercise class could be a potential powder keg containing any number of these scenarios. Consider, ultimately, the fact that the only common denominator among students in any given class you are teaching is simply their desire to be there. Your class will most likely contain a cross section of races, ethnicities, religions, ages, socio-economic levels, education, political beliefs, physical ability . . . you name it. How are you going to juggle all of that? How will you minimize any potential triggers that may cause a reaction in you?

The best answer comes from Don Miguel Ruiz, author of *The Four Agreements: A practical Guide to Personal Freedom*, a book I highly recommend you read. First published in 1997 by Amber-Allen Publishing, this book has sold around five million copies and has been translated into thirty-eight languages. In it, Don Miguel advocates personal freedom from beliefs and agreements that we have made with ourselves and others that are creating limitation and unhappiness in our lives. This philosophy comes from the Toltecs, a civilization dating back to A.D. 900 in what is now Mexico. The Toltecs were great teachers of spirituality, who viewed the universe as a complex energy system that is neither good nor bad. It just is. The ancient Naguals (shamans) of the Toltec Wisdom understood the illusionary nature of reality and used the universal laws of nature to create a life based on unconditional love and self-discovery. For thousands of years, these teachings were kept secret among the descendants of the ancient Toltecs until Don Miguel made them public in his book.

Personally, what struck me about the Agreements is their simplicity and that this ancient philosophy is as relevant today as it was thousands of years ago. It seems like human nature remains constant in spite of the evolution of our societies.

Let's dive into the wisdom of these Agreements, as they are an excellent compass to help you navigate the diverse personalities of the many people you are likely to encounter.

In Chapter 1, I asked you to imagine the students in your class carrying a small leather suitcase containing their blueprint, values, filters, and self-image neatly packed inside. Go back to that visual. Knowing what we know about the complexities of our personalities and that each of us carries our own individual set of personality patterns; let's examine how "The Four Agreements" would apply to how we might react to what's packed inside someone's suitcase.

Here they are:

"Don't Take Anything Personally"

The question is: "What could possibly be inside someone else's suitcase that has to do with us personally (unless we put it in there)?"

I have two little rescue dogs. One is an 8-year-old Yorkie mix who weighs about twelve pounds. Her name is Coqui and I adore her. She has a beautiful, sensitive heart. She bonds strongly with people; she is obedient, affectionate, and playful. Coqui is a really sweet and loving pup . . . UNLESS someone whom she doesn't know approaches to try to pet her. Her anxiety kicks in, she becomes fearful and she growls, snapping a warning and she may even lunge at the stranger to scare them away—all twelve pounds of her. It most always takes the friendly stranger by surprise. Some people shake it off, don't take it personally and will step back. But others react very differently. They become offended. Their feelings are hurt, they feel rejected and worse, some people think that dogs only show aggressive behavior towards "bad" people. I've heard the statement: "I'm a good person! Your dog should not have growled at me!"

Coqui has a story. The first year of her life was not good. She was born in a puppy mill that was massively breeding small "designer" dogs, selling them for upwards of $500 depending on the breed. In Coqui's case, something went wrong when her mother was bred. She did not turn out to be the Yorkie/Bichon that was expected. Her coat was too wiry; her body was out of proportion for the length of her legs. She was a ragamuffin puppy that was not so cute. Nobody wanted her. At about two or three months old, living inside a crate, Coqui had been passed over many times and with each passing month, her physical and emotional condition deteriorated, progressively

> **"What could possibly be inside someone else's suitcase that has to do with us personally (unless we put it in there)?**

lessening her chances of being adopted (much less purchased). The breeders gave up on her and began rationing her food. She became neglected and under-fed living in her excrement. Isolated and unsocialized, she began gnawing off patches of her fur and displaying aggressive behavior towards anyone who approached her crate. Puppy mills are not a permanent home for dogs. If they don't sell, they become a liability. They are either given away or euthanized. In Coqui's case, it was decided she was to be put down.

Coqui was rescued by a compassionate man who spotted her the day before she was scheduled to be euthanized. He couldn't care for her but took her home anyway, hoping to find her a loving home. Coqui came to live with me when she was about a year old. I do my best for her. I love her deeply. I care for her, look out for her, have worked with several trainers and even with a dog therapist to help her overcome her fear and anxiety. It's a work in progress which I will never abandon. She means that much to me.

When someone takes her anxiety personally, I typically explain that she is a rescue dog and has tremendous anxiety surrounding people she doesn't know. I try to smooth it over. But, in these instances, I often think about the First Agreement. In any given day, if you're aware, you will encounter multiple examples of people taking things personally when they otherwise shouldn't. Truth is, how can any of us know why someone may say a certain thing or behave in a certain way? If we can let go of thinking that everything happening around us has to do with us personally, we create a space for compassion and empathy to appear within us and our feelings are less likely to be hurt because we realize that what just happened did not have anything to do with us.

"Don't Make Assumptions"

The suitcase is closed, are you going to assume you know what's inside? There's a famous story called "The Man on the Subway". It's from the book *The 7 Habits of Highly Effective People: Powerful Lessons in Personal Change*, by Stephen R. Covey, (Simon and Schuster, 1990). This story beautifully illustrates this point. It goes like this:

> *I remember a mini-paradigm shift I experienced one Sunday morning on a subway in New York. People were sitting quietly – some reading newspapers, some lost in thought, some resting with their eyes closed. It was a calm, peaceful scene.*
>
> *Then suddenly, a man and his children entered the subway car. The children were so loud and rambunctious that instantly the whole climate changed. The man sat down next to me and closed his eyes, apparently oblivious to the situation. The children were yelling back and forth, throwing things, even grabbing people's papers. It was very disturbing. And yet, the man sitting*

next to me did nothing.

It was difficult not to feel irritated. I could not believe that he could be so insensitive as to let his children run wild like that and do nothing about it, taking no responsibility at all. It was easy to see that everyone else on the subway felt irritated, too. So finally, with what I felt like was unusual patience and restraint, I turned to him and said, "Sir, your children are really disturbing a lot of people. I wonder if you couldn't control them a little more?"

The man lifted his gaze as if to come to a consciousness of the situation for the first time and said softly, "Oh, you're right. I guess I should do something about it. We just came from the hospital where their mother died about an hour ago. I don't know what to think, and I guess they don't know how to handle it either."

Can you imagine what I felt at that moment? My paradigm shifted. Suddenly I saw things differently, and because I saw differently, I thought differently, I felt differently, I behaved differently. My irritation vanished. I didn't have to worry about controlling my attitude or my behavior; my heart was filled with the man's pain. Feelings of sympathy and compassion flowed freely. "Your wife just died? Oh I'm so sorry! Can you tell me about it? What can I do to help?" Everything changed in an instant. (30–31)

I believe our natural tendency to quickly size up a situation and have judgment around it is hardwired into our self-preservation and survival reflexes. It's not always off the mark. There are instances when we are in danger and must decide to fight or to flee. These are circumstances when assumptions can save our life. However, in everyday living we often find ourselves in situations that are unpleasant, irritating or inconsiderate, rude even . . . and we react. We may not realize we are in reactionary mode until new information comes in that reframes what we are perceiving—as evidenced and beautifully illustrated in this story. In an ideal reality, we would be able to slow down our reactionary responses until we have gathered as much information as possible. How do we interrupt our assumptions? We do so by being aware that we make them. We cannot assume what goes on inside people's minds unless they tell us. Until they do, we should not make any assumptions.

"Be Impeccable with Your Word"

Being impeccable with our word has more to do with thinking before we speak, than solely with conducting ourselves with the integrity of doing what we say we'll do. In the words of Shirdi Sai Baba (Hindu/Muslim spiritual master (1835-1918)): "Before you speak, ask yourself: Is it kind, is it true, is it necessary, does it improve upon the silence?" This Agreement can be the easiest one to embrace. The sheer act of having it present in our awareness, makes it possible. Not taking things personally and not making assumptions takes practice. But this Agreement only requires a declaration on our behalf to live out of this principle: To say only what champions others, to hold others large and not small, to be kind and compassionate, and to speak about others only in a manner that contributes to them positively. As a teacher, you may be critical of a student but only if the criticism is productive feedback that enables him or her to improve. Otherwise, the criticism may just be unkind . . . and unnecessary.

"Always Do Your Best"

This is where I can get a bit preachy because I have strong feelings about this. I mean, life is too short and too precious to live in mediocrity or to do things half way or half heartedly. Give your best to your life because only in doing so, do we make our lives count. Nothing wonderful ever comes out of anything less than someone's best . . . unless it is a fluke and who wants to gamble on that? Give your best to your class and it may grow.

❝ If we put our best into everything we do, it sets the stage for great things to happen... and eventually they will.

More classes may be offered to you. You may get a raise. You may earn enough income to make a living doing something you love to do! All good things!

These Four Agreements provide a strategy that can help us reign in our reactionary impulses enough to where we become less sensitive to something that is said or done that may set us off. This doesn't mean we don't feel the sting (albeit minimized). We are likely to remain sensitive; however, we may discover, upon embracing these principles that our threshold of tolerance can expand.

When we leave our homes every morning, we step into a world of stimuli. The hustle and bustle of life swirls around us and people step onto our path. We interact and move on. We give –we receive, we speak–we hear, we touch–we feel, we look–we are seen. . . in a perpetual circle of input and output. Keeping these Agreements present can be very helpful in minimizing spontaneous reactions by enabling us to hold a space for others which contains less judgment and more acceptance. They also help us emerge intact. Life can be a battleground; with the greatest casualties being those who journey through it taking everything personally or not understanding why the minimum effort they put out doesn't yield the success they crave.

Hold these Agreements close to your heart and you will set an example for others. Attitude and behavior are contagious. In the words of Mahatma Gandhi: *"Be the change that you wish to see in the world. As a man changes his own nature, so does the attitude of the world change towards him. This is the divine mystery supreme. A wonderful thing it is and the source of our happiness. We need not wait to see what others do."*

Five

"You do you, and I'll do me."
– Jason Mraz

Our half of the Equation

*W*e've taken a look at the complex configuration of patterns that meld together to give definition to our personalities. We've looked at how we react to the world and we've examined a strategy to help us put things into perspective. Now let's take a look at the final piece: our communication with others.

One of the blurriest lines in communication is the one that separates what we mean to say from what the other person hears. When we speak we believe we are being understood (unless there is feedback to the contrary) and when we are listening we assume we are understanding what the other person is communicating, and vice-versa. In reality, the most untrue statement anyone can say to another is: "I know exactly what you mean!" How could we? Every sentence anyone utters is influenced by his or her very own and private:

1. Imagery
2. Blueprint characteristics, values and filters
3. Circumstanial influences
4. Past experiences
5. Emotional state
6. Self-image

This dynamic is silently present on both sides of any conversation and leaves us a bit in the dark about what the other person is truly feeling or how he/she has actually interpreted what we are saying. Once we come to accept this truth, what is next? Where does this leave us? If we cannot accurately perceive how another person has interpreted our message; if we have no control over another person's hidden filters and influences, how can we ensure he/she interprets what we are communicating in accordance with our intention?

The answer is: we cannot. We can only be responsible for what Don Miguel Ruiz refers to as "our 50 percent". In his book, *The Mastery of Love: A Practical Guide to the Art of Relationship (Hay House Incorporated, 2003)*, he establishes that no one can, nor should, take responsibility for how another person interprets what is being said. The Agreement that suggests we should be impeccable with our word only refers to the person speaking, not the person listening. We should strive to be kind and speak truthfully to the best of our ability, while also accepting that we are not responsible for how another interprets our message.

This is especially important for those of us who come into frequent contact with people we don't know very well. It's easier to have our antenna up around our friends and family (with whom we have history and may be aware of triggers that set them off), but with others, the landmines are typically hidden from view.

I recall a student of mine who was profoundly dedicated to her dance studies. She attended classes regularly and would often push herself beyond her ability by taking classes that were above her level. She wanted to improve and to be the best dancer she could be. I greatly admired her. I could relate to her desire for growth. One day, in casual conversation, I complimented her for being such an ambitious dancer. A few days later, she pulled me aside to tell me she did not appreciate being called "ambitious" and why did I say such a thing? She was really upset with me! I immediately apologized and explained to her that I meant it as a compliment. But she insisted that it wasn't. So I asked her what about being ambitious did she see as negative? She replied that she believed ambitious people were ruthlessly aggressive and would plow over anyone to get what they

> **We should strive to be kind and speak truthfully to the best of our ability, while also accepting that we are not responsible for how another interprets our message.**

wanted. She went on to say that she is not like that and did not want to be categorized as being that kind of person. To her, "ambitious" was an insult.

I didn't argue my point of view with her, nor did I try to change her mind about her definition of ambitious. I did not become defensive and I also didn't beat myself up for "insulting" a student I valued greatly. I accepted it and I let it go. I knew I had been kind and sincere with my words, and that is all I can be responsible for. I also never mentioned the word "ambitious" to her again!

If we are able to decline responsibility for how others perceive our words, we can experience much greater lightness in how we communicate. Communicating from a place of paranoia over how someone may interpret what we say is a heavy burden to carry. My general rule of thumb is: If it comes from a place of love, let it rip. If it doesn't, then think it through and strive to deliver the message through a filter of kindness and empathy—to the best of your ability.

Do your best with this knowledge. At the end of the day, you must take care of yourself. As a teacher, you will come into contact with many diverse souls (I keep saying this for a reason!) that are dealing with who knows what in their lives. You are not responsible for what anyone in your class is struggling with. Accept responsibility for your 50 percent and let the rest of it go.

Six

Nonverbal communication is an elaborate secret
code that is written nowhere, known by none,
and understood by all."
– Edward Sapir

Reception:
Listening to What Your Students Are
Not Telling/Telling You

*S*o much about what people say . . . What about what they
don't say? Communication is believed to be 7 percent verbal
(words) and 93 percent non-verbal (body language, facial expressions).
While in class, your students are constantly communicating with
you—only it may not be verbal. You're getting that 93 percent and
your ability to receive the messages your students are sending is
directly correlated to the class experience you are creating. If you
ignore the messages your class will feel disconnected, but, if you
respond to the messages, you create an atmosphere of inclusion.

Body language and facial expressions can speak volumes if
we are paying attention. Oftentimes in class, this may be our greatest

source of information. Are our students smiling or are they looking out the window? Do they have a strained look on their faces? Or worse, are they smiling but their body language is sending a different message altogether? Not sure about it . . . you may ask: "Does anyone have any questions?" They may say no (when clearly they do). "Should we move on or repeat the movement?" Silence. We may ask, but we are actually already being told.

Everything we need to know about a student in class, he or she communicates to us physically— but we must be aware and our lens must be clear. It is through the observation of these nonverbal messages that we can gain a strong foothold on what is happening around us and decide whether or not we should make an adjustment in what we're doing (because we should not rely on our students to verbally tell us—although some may). Do we hold a stretch longer, repeat a choreographic sequence, speed things up or slow them down? If we are observant, we will know—without asking.

To increase the likelihood of an accurate "read" on non-verbal cues, we begin by silencing our mental chatter to allow information to easily flow in. Mind chatter hinders and often obstructs incoming information, making it very difficult to listen to or pay attention to someone else. Simply asking the voice in our mind to be silent or attempting to drown it out by cranking up the volume on the stereo is not a fool proof strategy. Willing our minds to calm down is rarely effective and using music to distract us only works occasionally. Worse, all this effort may cause us to lose focus on our students. The best "mind quieting" strategy I have discovered is to create a context for achieving this mental state through the implementation of environmental triggers and behavioral rituals that set the stage for this to happen. Let me explain.

The Creative Habit: Learn It and Use It for Life (Simon & Schuster, 2006) by the great contemporary choreographer Twyla Tharpe is a largely autobiographical book for dancers and choreographers about making creativity a habit. This was my first introduction to the concept of trigger - ritual - reward. In her book, Twyla writes that creativity is not something that can be called up on demand and that the best strategy for inviting it to appear is to engage in a daily ritual that gets your creative process going. Stravinsky played

> **" Everything we need to know about a student, he or she communicates to us physically— but we must be aware and our lens must be clear.**

the same fugue by Bach every morning while he was composing. Her ritual is a bit more detailed.

On the days in which she must create choreography, she would follow a ritual that communicated to her subconscious mind what she was preparing to do. She would wake up at a specific hour, eat a specific breakfast, wear a specific outfit, and she'd take a taxi (never the subway) to the studio. Once there, she'd turn on her music and fold herself into a fetal position in the middle of the floor imagining she was inside an egg. Her movement would then begin as she visualized herself breaking through the shell and into life. These steps were repeated exactly (with no deviation) on every morning she was headed into the studio to create movement.

> **" I was able to use this knowledge to create new desired outcomes for myself, including to being able to fully present and in receptor mode for my students.**

Author Charles Duhigg, in his book: *The Power of Habit: Why We Do What We Do in Life and Business (Random House, 2012)* describes a similar triangle of Cue ➡ Routine ➡ Reward

It looks like this:

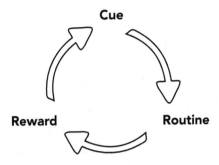

Mr. Duhigg argues that in order to achieve a specific outcome, we must engage in a series of actions that we have conditioned our minds to associate with that desired outcome. For example: Think of your bedtime routine. Notice three things you do before you get in bed for the night. Do you tend to do them in the same order? These three actions are signaling to your brain that it's time to go to sleep. If you interrupt this routine, you are likely to take longer to fall asleep. We don't need to look too far to notice all the routines that make up our days. For me, that was the most powerful take away from this book. I had never realized just how many routines I had going on within a normal day cycle and once I made the connection between my everyday automatic routines and Twyla's deliberate routine, I was able to use this knowledge to create new desired outcomes for myself, including being able to be fully present and in receptor mode for my students.

This is my routine: It begins when I walk into my class. I weave through the room, greeting everyone (or as many people as possible depending on the size of the class). By the time I reach the music console and plug in my electronics I am fully present in the space with everyone who is there. I begin to let go of what separates me from those present by thinking of myself as a conduit: a clean slate, in service to them. At the start of every class:

1. I "clear" my mind—by focusing on my breath.
2. I become present in the moment—by noticing how my body feels, the floor beneath my feet.
3. I establish a connection to the music—by feeling the beat and rhythm of the composition.
4. I focus on inclusion—by visualizing a large net that originates from me to include everyone present.
5. I connect with the joy and privilege of being able to do what I am about to do.

For me, the "cue" is walking into my class, the "ritual" is the five steps listed above and the "reward" is my ability to perceive and receive non-verbal communication from my students while being absent of judgment and in complete acceptance.

Great teaching requires this level of connectivity and this connection must be made at the very beginning—not mid-way through. The opportunity to "stop the train once it leaves the station" (when a class begins) is a luxury not typically available when we are teaching thirty or more people in a class. Interrupting a class because we do not have a "pulse" on what is going on around us will kill the class's momentum, creating a "choppy" experience of starts and stops for our students. If you have thirty students in your class, imagine the class as one piece with thirty moving parts rather than thirty distinctly separate pieces. Creating a connection with a group of individuals requires us to become "invisible" while fully present and connected to our awareness, so to speak. And when we achieve this, it's an indescribable feeling that can send us virtually onto a spiritual plane.

To develop your own cue and ritual for quieting your mind, notice what you do in the first few minutes after you step into your classroom. Try to repeat this exact behavior in your next class and every class from then on. Set the intention (ask the universe) to quiet your thoughts before you engage in this ritual. Eventually the ritual will stick and your sub conscious will make the connection between the cue, the ritual and the outcome you desire.

> ## The quieter you become, the more you can hear. –Tony Moorcroft

Seven

"It's not about whether we judge, but about how."
– Ofelia de La Valette

The Right and Wrong Kinds of Judgment

*F*or the purpose of this teacher training, I would like to introduce you to three general types of judgment:

1. One is based upon data
2. One is based upon assumptions
3. The third is based upon intuition

If we ask a student to perform a particular movement and he/she doesn't properly execute it, we may make an overall constructive, critical judgment about the non-execution that is based upon that student's physical limitations (data). Or we may think he/she just isn't trying hard enough—this is assumptive judgment. Intuitive judgment is based upon our awareness of how someone feels.

Let's examine these in more detail:

Data based judgment is fairly straightforward. It's solution driven. A student winces every time he/she bends his/her left knee. The knee is compromised because of an injury or a medical condition. A student slips and falls out of a yoga pose. You notice he/she doesn't have a mat. A student stumbles through your Turns and Leaps Jazz class who's wearing the wrong type of shoes. A brand new student who is unfamiliar with your class takes his/her place on the floor directly behind you, blocking your view of the class (and that of the class of you). A student arrives late and/or leaves early... Any one of these situations is disruptive to a class. However, using data based judgment you can address the issue with certainty. You may give modification around the injured knee, you may give your student a yoga mat, and you may change your position in the front of the class so not only the new student feels secure, but everyone else can see you as well. You can ask your Turns class student to dance in his/her socks, and you may say a prayer of gratitude for that over-scheduled soul who is struggling to do something for himself/herself—attending half a class is better than no attendance at all. These are all reactions based on data judgment.

Assumptive judgment is also pretty straightforward, only this type of judgment has absolutely no productive value in the classroom or anywhere else in life for that matter. It is so absent of any sound analytical processes that it is typically, if not most always, wrong. Regardless if it's negative or positive in tone, either way it's a waste of thought. It's pure conjecture. It can also falsely accuse, label or punish someone. Here is an example of assumptive judgment: Imagine that same student who winces every time they bend their left knee . . . an assumptive judgment may be that the student is lazy and trying to look like they have an excuse not to do the exercise. Assumptive judgment requires us to make up a story in our head, any story that suits us which allows us to explain a situation. It is often accusatory. This type of judgment is toxic, and if you ever catch yourself doing it, stop immediately! Stick to data-based, solution-driven judgment. Or, take a stab at intuitive judgment — which is the jewel in the crown.

> **We can successfully teach using judgment based upon data, but if we are able to tap into our intuitive judgment, we will profoundly touch our students.**

Intuition is often referred to as a "gut" feeling, a knowing of sorts. Many would argue our intuition is dialed into a greater source of information—tapping into a pervasive realm of awareness. With **intuitive judgment** there is no story attached: it is a feeling. To access our intuitive judgment we must check in with how we feel about something once we've cleared out our reactionary patterns of response. In other words, ask yourself: What is my gut telling me? Then subtract out your patterns so you remove your prejudices from the equation and see what shows up. Intuitive judgment is the most powerful tool a teacher can have. It is devoid of self-doubt and allows us to operate at a greater, more inclusive level that envelops everyone present.

The first step in developing intuitive judgment is to be aware it exists and how it is different from the other two. Of the three judgments, the least effective in teaching is the assumptive one. So go ahead and toss that one out. We can successfully teach using judgment based upon data, but if we are able to tap into our intuitive judgment, we will profoundly touch our students. They will grow beyond expectation as a direct result of our leadership and guidance.

As discussed in the previous chapter, to establish an environment in which intuitive judgment is possible, we first must set the stage by connecting with each student prior to the start of class. This is another good reason to take a moment to walk through the room and make eye contact with each individual. Depending on the number of students, there may be time for a verbal greeting. Otherwise, a smile or a non-verbal acknowledgement is sufficient. Of the 400 billion bits of information per second that reach the brain, only 2,000 bits are utilized. This means more information is registered in our subconscious than in our conscious mind. A simple walk around your classroom will collect an enormous amount of information about who is present, including the energy their soul contributes to the group dynamic. This is food for intuitive judgment.

I have discovered that I am able to tap into my intuitive judgment by watching everyone in my class through my peripheral vision. What's happening in my periphery is a blur of cohesive movement that allows my mind to go directly to what is not moving in unison. This tells me where there's a disconnection, enabling me to address it. I direct my attention to this area of the room to where I can identify what is "off". This lets me uncover what part or sequence of the movement I am teaching needs additional instruction or repetition. I will have no internal conversation about why this is happening nor hold any judgment about the individual(s) who may be struggling. This is a teaching strategy we will cover in greater detail in the second part of this book. For now, suffice to know this teaching approach is tied to intuitive judgment.

The most important take away from this chapter is to become aware that there are different types of judgment: effective (data based), ineffective (assumptive) and ideal (intuitive). Data based judgment is individualized and solution driven. Assumptive judgment can inhibit a student's growth by making up justifications for their limitation (and therefore holding them "small" and not championing their potential). Intuitive judgment is ideal because it envelops everyone cohesively and keeps the class moving along. A clear understanding of these different types of judgment will enable you to be aware of how you are processing and responding to incoming information.

Eight

"Connection is the energy that is created between people when they feel seen, heard, and valued; when they can give and receive without judgment."
–Brene Brown

The Power of Acknowledgment

*A*nother significant reason to take a moment in order to make a connection with our students is to show gratitude for their presence. In today's hectic world of layered obligations and responsibilities, we never know what obstacles our students have had to overcome just to get to class. Terrible traffic, cell phones beeping or ringing, appointments that must be kept, a sleepless night, even a crippling depression . . . any number of occurrences can get in the way of making the trip across town to class. For every person who made it to class, there may be five more who didn't. Making it to class is an accomplishment for many and when they arrive, no one likes to feel invisible. It is important to acknowledge those who made it and let them know we're happy they are there. Please take a moment to truly contemplate this. Many of the people standing in our class went to great lengths to be there. Consequently, we must honor their effort with gratitude for their presence.

I'd like to introduce you to Kevin M, a truly exceptional teacher. I've known Kevin for more than two decades, having first met him when he subbed a cardio funk class I was taking at a gym in Atlanta in 1995. So great was the impression he made on me, that I found out where he was teaching and followed him there. Nine years later when I opened dance 101, I hunted him down to invite him to teach classes at the studio. Unfortunately, his schedule had no openings at the time, so I made a note to contact him again in a year. This went on for the next seven years—I courted that man until the stars and moon aligned and he accepted. Imagine that! Imagine being such a successful and popular teacher that a studio owner would call you relentlessly for seven years until you said yes.

What does Kevin do that sets him apart? How does he create his particular class experience that draws in so many people?

For starters, Kevin is a gifted performer and choreographer. He worked professionally as a dancer during his twenties and thirties, so he has the experience, talent, and training to teach a great dance class. Additionally, he once owned and operated an entertainment company and worked as a DJ, so he understands the importance of keeping people engaged and entertained, and the playlists he puts together are amazing. In his classes he melds these elements together to create a unique experience that is dance, but also entertainment and connection.

> **Many of the people standing in our class went to great lengths to be there. Consequently, we must honor their effort with gratitude for their presence.**

He begins his class with a greeting. He welcomes everyone, he smiles at everyone (a smile that never quits) and he connects on a personal level with the group. By the time he walks over to turn on the music to kick off the class, virtually everyone present feels seen and appreciated. He instructs everyone to have fun, not to worry about the steps, to let go, and just move to the music.

Kevin teaches his choreography and dances with the class until he's confident everyone has learned the movement and can do it without following him. This is when the magic happens. He steps away from the front and begins to weave in, out and around each individual, taking this opportunity to really connect—to come into each person's "personal space", make eye contact, tap their shoulder, smile, laugh, and dance with them. He hoots and yells, and laughs loudly. At times he'll playfully confuse students into a wrong step or lead them to the right when they should go left . . . and lets out a hearty laugh. He entertains by creating an interactive environment where everyone feels that they are a part of the "show". Kevin's magic touch is in the way he combines acknowledgment with entertainment. The fact that everyone sweats up a storm and gets a great workout is really only the icing on the cake, although that may be the initial reason a new student may decide to take his class.

Kevin's choreography is fun, easy to learn, and repetitive, but that's not the reason people flock to his classes. They come for how he makes them *feel*. I've watched Kevin teach to hundred people in a 3,000 square foot space and connect with every person present. If he misses someone during class, he'll connect with him/her afterwards. No one leaves his class without feeling acknowledged, seen, appreciated, and entertained. It's a winning formula that resonates and lands with many people. Some of his students have been with him for over a decade, which is a phenomenal accomplishment in the exercise industry. His success has less to do with content (his choreography) than it does with delivery and connection. This further supports my belief that what you teach is very important but is secondary to how you teach.

If we focus on connecting, the teaching naturally follows. In the words of Maya Angelou:

> **At the end of the day people won't remember what you said or did, they will remember how you made them feel.**

Acknowledge your students. Make them feel special and appreciated and the magic will happen in your class as well.

Nine

"Coming together is a beginning; keeping together is progress: working together is success."
–Henry Ford

Fulfilling Expectations

When I began my dance studies in 1995, there was only one studio in town that offered adult "open" classes. Delighted to have found this studio, I signed up for beginner classes. Note: "open" means open to drop in, as in anybody can take any class regardless of level or prior training. There was no system in place to qualify a student for any particular class level. Whichever class you wanted to take was available to you. The studio relied on the judgment of its adult students, giving them complete responsibility for their decision to take any particular class. Further, the studio encouraged teachers to teach to the level of the majority of students in class—regardless of the advertised level of that class.

This created an atmosphere of unpredictability for me. I'd

arrive to take a beginner hip hop class only to find myself over my head in an advanced class because that was the overall level of most of the students in that class on that day. As a result and over time, I became adept at predicting the level of any particular class by surveying who was present. Had I had other options for classes, I would not have continued my studies at that studio. It was extremely stressful to have such a chaotic educational arch. I did manage to learn what I needed eventually; however, I am a very determined person. Most people would have become discouraged . . . and many did.

Much has been written about the success of McDonald's restaurants. Many attribute its popularity to the consistency of their products and how well the company succeeds in fulfilling their customer's expectations. Their customers know exactly what they are going to get when they place their order. Approach your class with this understanding.

What do your students expect from you? This may sound obvious and unworthy of mention, but twenty-five years of teaching and managing teachers has taught **" Nobody wants a cheeseburger when they order a chicken sandwich.** me otherwise. Without respect for students' expectations, I've watched countless talented teachers deliver unfocused classes that were all over the place in level and content.

While you may have a list of what you expect from your students (no gum chewing, no cell phones, no talking over you, be engaged, work hard, make it count, etc.), make no mistake your students also have their expectations of you. These expectations come mainly from two sources:

1. How the class is described in its advertising, and . . .
2. What others are saying about your class.

While it may be more difficult to have access to what other students are saying, your class description should be readily available for you to read. You must be absolutely aware of its content and you should read it, not just once, but periodically. Classes evolve. Today's beginner class may slowly creep up to be an intermediate level without you even noticing. This is especially true if you have established a strong regular following. Students will improve considerably, especially those who are consistent in their attendance.

I suggest you read your class description every five to six months. If you feel the class is moving at a higher level, notify your studio management. Your class description may need to be either rewritten or you may need to bring the class back to the original description. One or the other. Ignoring the evolutionary dynamic of your class could eventually cause it to stagnate and ultimately die. Growth is the oxygen of business. If you and your class are not attracting and capturing the enthusiasm of new students, your class will not survive.

Teaching a class that is different than its description is a silent class killer. As my daughter Paulina says: "Nobody wants a cheeseburger when they order a chicken sandwich." If you have deviated from your published description, you are most likely sabotaging your success. Students experience confusion, frustration and sometimes even anger when they receive something different than what they were expecting (and paid for). Most commonly they will simply not return to your class, especially if they have other options. Or they may blast you, and/or the studio, on a review site using statements like: "That studio/teacher is deceptive! They advertise a beginner class that is advanced! I felt so stupid! I'm never going back! ONE STAR! Don't go there!" Neither of these options is desirable and both could have been avoided.

Your ability to retain new students is a critical aspect to the long term success of your class. Students cycle in and out; this is a fact. You will not likely retain your regulars forever. People move, get attached to new things, have children, priorities change, they may sustain an injury, illness etc. You may have students that remain with you for years, but this is a very small percentage. Most will not. Today's new student is tomorrow's regular. Always cultivate that! If you wish to build a long term teaching career, you must constantly welcome new students into your classes!

In addition to teaching the great class that is expected and eagerly welcoming new students and inviting them back, your students are a great source of valuable information that can help you perfect your class experience. Ask your new students if they heard about your class from someone. What did they hear? What about the description convinced them to come? Do they have a specific goal in mind? Was the class what they expected? How your new students respond to questions like these will help you identify any hidden aspects of your class experience which may potentially sabotage your success. Listen very carefully to what they say! Make adjustments where necessary, whether in the class description or to the class itself!

> **Your ability to retain new students is a critical aspect to the long term success of your class.**

In a highly competitive market, your class must be on point. The great news is: Now that you are aware of it, the mastery of it is simple. A successful win-win outcome is when your planned delivery matches the expectation of your students!

Ten

"People don't buy what you do; they buy why you do it.
And what you do simply proves what you believe."
–Simon Sinek

Developing Confidence

I often think about how the classroom is such a great metaphor for life. As everything we do, when a teacher enters her classroom, everything about her demeanor, her gate, her appearance, her facial expressions, and what she says when she greets her class sets the tone, influencing her student's expectations about what might happen in the next hour. We communicate confidence from a source deep within that springs from our knowing that we are prepared and have a purpose to fulfill.

Preparedness + Purpose = Confidence

Preparedness

My daughter Paulina is the best gift-giver I know. She loves giving gifts. It's a real thrill for her. When my birthday approaches, she begins thinking and planning what she will get for me weeks ahead of time. Once she decides on what the actual gift will be, she begins brainstorming on how she will package and wrap it. It doesn't stop there. She searches for the perfect card that not only relates to the occasion or to the gift, but also nails my sense of humor. She uses colorful pens to elaborately write my name on the card and may add sticky jewels or some other mixed media detail to adorn the card. The gift, the presentation, the wrapping, and the card are each carefully thought out. When she presents her gift to me, she is confident that I am going to love it. Her excitement about giving the gift to me not only enhances my joy in receiving it but also makes the exchange a two-way participatory celebration of the occasion. She enjoys my birthday as much as I do!

Take this scenario and apply it to your relationship with your students. You've put great thought and effort into preparing a class for them and are excited to present the material. They have made their way into your class and that is the occasion you are celebrating. Imagine your body language when you walk in! You might even greet your students by saying "Boy, am I excited about teaching this class today! I have something really special for you and I can't wait to show you what I've prepared!" What kind of tone would that set? If you were to regard every class as a gift to your students, how might you think they'd respond to you? And imagine what that would do for your confidence level!

The amount of time, thought, and effort you put into creating your class experience will either increase or decrease your level of confidence in teaching it. The more time you prepare, the more confident you will be. Subject matter expertise may provide a solid foundation for a good class, but greatness is expressed in the delivery.

Do not confuse the two. Being skilled in your content is absolutely necessary, but that alone may not generate the level of confidence that comes from knowing you are prepared. If you've put time into carefully selecting your music and have planned your content, if you've given thought to and tailored your warm-up to prepare the body for your specific sequence of movement and you've set specific goals and objectives you intend to accomplish during the hour, you will have fully outlined your purpose: This is putting 100 percent into your 50 percent.

Make time and commit to carefully prepare your class and your confidence will soar. You'll walk into the room excited about the gift you're about to give and that excitement will tag everyone present. From a student perspective, there is no greater joy than to be taught by someone who is passionate, prepared and excited to teach what he/she knows. This is the absolute ideal.

However, sometimes the ideal is not possible and on occasion you may find yourself in an unexpected situation in which you must pull a rabbit out of the hat and teach a class you did not prepare for. I have a recent example of this that happened to me just a few weeks ago. I walked out of my 10:30 a.m. class to discover that the teacher who followed me at 11:30 a.m. had not yet arrived at the studio. The front desk asked me to step in, and of course I agreed. When I walked into the classroom, there were a number of students waiting and ready to move. It was an intermediate level Contemporary class—a dance genre and level I am not qualified to teach. In fact, there were students present who had much more contemporary training than I did (which is close to none) who

> **The amount of time, thought, and effort you put into creating your class experience will either increase or decrease your level of confidence in teaching it.**

might have taught a great class had they been asked. Unfortunately this idea did not come to me in that moment. I walked in with zero confidence in my ability to teach that class. But, I also walked in with tremendous confidence in my ability to make the best of the situation, to the extent of my limitations on the subject matter.

Based upon my years of teaching and life experience, I can confidently share with you a few triggers that will absolutely upset virtually anybody:

1. People do not like being deceived, lied to, or disrespected.
2. People do not like wasting their money.
3. People do not like wasting their time.

And here's another important truth: It is impossible to fool someone who knows more about a subject than you do. I guarantee you that five minutes into the class, the most advanced students present would already know how little I knew about the subject matter. I knew this going in. I wasn't going to fool anyone and I wasn't going to try (that would have been so disrespectful!).

Here's what I did: I embraced the situation with complete transparency and authenticity. I explained that the teacher had not arrived, that I was asked to step in and that I was committed to doing the best job I could for them. I told them that I was not trained in Contemporary and that my only qualification for teaching this class was the fact that I was present and willing to help out. I asked them for their help, suggesting we all collaborate on the creation of the choreography and they accepted! I improvised the first few eight counts of movement to get us started then watched how they responded. I noticed how they inserted a jump instead of my leg lift and a double turn in place of my single. I incorporated these non-verbal suggestions and together we created what turned out to be a really lovely Contemporary piece!

Asking the students for their collaboration defined the experience of the class as giving them an opportunity to explore their own ability for creating movement. And in this regard, I was able to contribute a valuable learning experience. Had I not been transparent in my approach to the class, I would have likely succeeded in disappointing most everyone present. Wonderful things can happen when we expose our vulnerability and ask for help. People rally around that! It can replace the thought: "This person seems uncomfortable teaching; they must not enjoy it", with: "Wow this person is courageous! It can't be easy teaching a class for the first time! I admire her!" Don't ever be afraid to communicate your vulnerability!

There are other scenarios in which you may feel the rug being pulled out from underneath you: You may be asked at the last minute to sub a class you are qualified to teach but you are not prepared for. Or you may come prepared to teach a certain class, only to find out there's been a miscommunication and you're expected to teach something different. These less than ideal situations can shake even the most confident among us.

The burning question is: How do we acquire and maintain an unshakable level of confidence in ourselves? Experience helps greatly, but that takes time. How do we circumvent time and acquire confidence now? The answer is we tap into the bigger picture: Purpose!

Purpose

Purpose is never "what" we do; it's always "why" we do it.

When my kids were little there were times when we had a particular outing planned that was not popular with one or the other. In these instances I used to say to them that it wasn't so much about "what" we were doing, as it was about spending time together (the "why"). When planning a dinner out with my closest girlfriends, my focus is being with them first, where we eat is secondary. These are great examples of how the "why" is different than the "what".

There are also instances when the "what" *is* the "why". My favorite travel destination is the Caribbean, and when I am able to travel there, where I stay, the food I eat, and the beautiful beaches I visit is the "why" I'm going there. However, when it comes to developing confidence, the "why" becomes more important than the "what". "Why", "what", "what", "why"? I bet your head is spinning.

Author, motivational speaker, and marketing consultant, Simon Sinek gave a very popular TED talk in 2009 entitled "*How Great Leaders Inspire Action*". Although presented in a business context, I believe the message applies beyond the boardroom. He calls it "The Golden Circle" and here is how it applies to teaching:

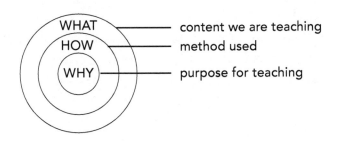

In an instructional fitness class, the "why" is our purpose for teaching, the "how" is the method we use and the "what" is the material we are teaching. All three are tremendously important and necessary in order to achieve excellence as a teacher. However, for this chapter I'd like to focus on the "why".

A clear vision of our "why" defines our purpose in teaching and impacts how we approach our classes. There are ideal "whys" and not so ideal "whys" to teach exercise or artistic movement.

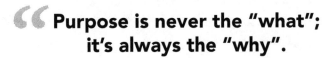

Purpose is never the "what"; it's always the "why".

Let's begin with a few ideal "whys":

1. I teach because it brings me joy to contribute to others.
2. I teach because I want to share my knowledge.
3. I teach because I want to bring joy into people's lives.
4. I teach because I want to share my enjoyment, love, and passion for what I love to do.

If you notice, four declarations have to do with giving and because all four originate in the heart, the intention is pure. While there are always exceptions to any rule, for the most part the gift of true giving instills clarity of purpose. It speaks not to the "what" or the "how" you are delivering the gift, but to its origins. If our "origin of purpose" is one of magnanimity and generosity, what we do flows through this filter and out into the world. Our "why" is communicated through non-verbal cues and lives in our energy field (which we personally can't perceive, but others can). It will also temper our thoughts about ourselves. If we know unequivocally that we teach because we thrive on championing others, confidence organically manifests in the execution of this kind of love.

As much as I'd like to affirm that everyone is perfect in their own way and to be true and authentic to yourself, I cannot overlook the landmines. There are certain "whys" that will not enhance your self-confidence nor likely will they help you build a long-term successful class. A few of these are:

1. I teach because I am bored taking other people's classes.
2. I teach because it's my workout.
3. I teach because I want people to validate how talented I am.
4. I teach because I want free classes at the studio.
5. I teach because it's a means to a selfish gain. (i.e., recruiting new personal training clients.)

All of these reasons have a self-centered origin. Whereas a clear vision of purpose is necessary to achieve self-confidence, self-motivated purpose breeds arrogance and entitlement and will only get you so far, until others around you figure it out. By and large, most people are repelled by arrogance once they've identified it. The point is: People respond enthusiastically to selfless intentions and if your "why" is defined by them, it will impact your classes in a very wonderful way.

Think about your "why". Write it down. Let it be your statement of purpose (much like a business has a mission statement) and let it guide you. Keep it present when you prepare your class and watch your confidence soar.

Eleven

"Kindness in words creates confidence.
Kindness in thinking creates profoundness.
Kindness in giving creates love."
–Lao Tzu

Acceptance: The Art of Connection

Our ability to connect with our students is EVERYTHING. In fact, our ability to connect with any of the people in our lives is the basis of all relationships. If we examine our relationships we find that acceptance is their determining common denominator. Whether good or bad, complicated or straightforward, acceptance is the foundation. Volumes of books have been written about this topic! But keep in mind; we are only looking at a specific slice . . . which is how it relates to teaching your class. Big topic, small slice! With that disclaimer out of the way, let's examine what acceptance means in a classroom setting.

Acceptance begins with acknowledgement. The people who have arrived to take your class did so as a result of various degrees of sacrifice. It's their day off and they have forgone time at the pool or a walk in the park to make it to your class. They live across town and have driven miles through traffic to arrive on time. They've sacrificed their lunch hour to be with you. They've overcome the intimidation factor of taking your class for the first time. Bottom line, your students have made an effort to be in your class . . . No exceptions!

Once you fully appreciate and acknowledge the presence of the beautiful souls in your class, the stage is set for you to accept that they are there for reasons you may or may not know. All you can know for certain is that they have come to learn or to practice with YOU. Acceptance is an attitude that embraces others like a virtual hug. It communicates a message of: "You are welcome here!"

In any given class, you will have students with varying levels of ability present. This happens even if your class is clearly described to be of a certain level. Please, you must, must, must accept this completely and not have any conversation in your mind whatsoever about why beginners are in your advanced class or why advanced students are in your beginner class. Every person present has his/her motives for being there. You may not know what they are. But, if you accept the wisdom of their decision, it will free you to deliver the class you had planned.

Acceptance does not mean altering your class in any way to accommodate what you think are the motives of those present. Acceptance is not bumping up or down the class level because of the ability level of who is present. Acceptance is embracing that whoever shows up has done so based upon the class description, its advertised level, what they've heard about the class or any number of other reasons you cannot possibly know. Altering the class experience to suit the ability level of who's present will sabotage the success of your class over time by shaking the confidence of your regulars in your willingness to deliver upon their expectations. Acceptance is giving others what we are there to deliver, not giving what we think they want—which might require all sorts of presumptions and assumptions. There's always the possibility that students might show up for your class without having taken the time to read about it. They might have an hour free and may simply want to take a class. But this is not on you; it's their decision. You cannot let their presence in class throw you off course. Accept their decision to be there and in the process you will establish an authentic connection.

> **Acceptance does not mean altering your class in any way to accommodate what you think are the motives of those present.**

One of the many things I love about yoga is how the Namaste-greeting is used to close a class. "Namaste" literally means "I bow to you" in Hindu. It is a gesture of acknowledgement of the soul in one by the soul in another. Typically, this gesture is expressed at the end of a practice but it can and sometimes is uttered at the beginning of a class as well. I encourage you to embrace the "spirit" of Namaste throughout your class, regardless of what you are teaching. Namaste is the embodiment of acceptance and the inevitable consequence of acceptance is connection.

Twelve

"Your vibe attracts your tribe"
–Anonymous

Find Your Voice and Your Tribe Will Find You

There are currently about forty-seven teachers on faculty at dance 101. On any given day we have thousands of visitors to our website searching for classes to take and many of them will select a class based solely on its description. This requires quite a bit of creative writing to convey the essence and feel of each class to someone who has never seen nor taken it.

We dream up imaginative class names and clever descriptions to spark interest. However, for all our creativity, the only true description of any one of our classes is to call them by what they really are: The Joy of Tap is actually best described as Barry and his students' tap class; Ballet Barre Fit is Lauren and her students' ballet class; King of Hearts is Jared and his students' hip hop class, etc. Each class is a community, a tribe, with the teacher front and center as its Pied Piper.

Earlier in Chapter 9: "Fulfilling Expectations", we discussed the importance of delivering a class to match its written description. However, it's important to make the distinction between a written description of a class and the "individual voice" of the teacher. Our "voice" is the instrument that colors the class experience and attracts individuals who are drawn to our essence, as well as to our content. Our "voices" appeal to like-minded "voices". This is one of the reasons teaching classes can be so tremendously fulfilling. Teachers naturally attract their ilk, many of whom will also be drawn to others in the circle. The desire for class content and knowledge may be the bait, but what brings students back over and over is the feeling of inclusion in the community that has sprouted from the teacher's voice.

❝❝ **What fuels your voice is your passion.**

Teaching from your "voice" is what makes your class special and unique. Teachers who teach from their "voices" create very personal class experiences that feel genuine and authentic to others. It's this desire for connection that brought the boutique fitness industry into being. Jason Kelly, New York bureau chief for Bloomberg, in his book *Sweat Equity: Inside the New Economy of Mind and Body (John Wiley & Sons, 2016)*, writes that Millennials (defined as those who were born between 1981 and 1997) seem to want experiences versus "things" and that fitness can satisfy the desire for togetherness and the need for deeper connection. But it's not just the Millennial generation, I assure you. I believe that in this age of digital and social media relationships, people of all ages want connection, and community.

Whenever a group of people assemble to engage in a shared experience, they want to be among friends, feel welcomed and relevant, and if this group is in your class, the students are looking to you to lead them into that experience. This means you have to show up—not just physically, but in every regard. Your personality must take front and center and you must be comfortable with that.

Finding our "voice" as teachers can take years to uncover unless we understand what drives it. Truthfully, the journey of self-discovery is actually the process of identifying what gives life to our essence. Let me save you a few years on this one . . . What fuels your voice is your passion.

Our "voice" is the instrument of our beliefs. It gives sound to the wave of non-verbal energy that touches anyone in our periphery and its volume is directly correlated to the intensity of our passion about the subject. I can't think of a better way to illustrate this than by asking you to take a moment and think about a TED talk you've recently watched. Choose any talk—because every single one is delivered by someone who is passionate about his/her message (hence the platform's popularity). Pull some of the talks up on your computer or phone and watch them . . . with the sound turned off. Observe the speakers' body language and facial expressions. Pay attention to how they stand, move their hands, shrug their shoulders, and lean into the audience when making a point. Notice how often they smile . . . After watching a few minutes, you will want to turn the volume back on! You've gotten a clear picture of their joy and excitement about having something important to share with you. How can you not be drawn into that? Every word they utter may be well crafted for their presentation but

> **Teachers naturally attract their ilk, many of whom will also be drawn to others in the circle.**

their body language begins every sentence with "I'm so excited to tell you...!!

Your voice will always be the loudest when you are teaching something you are passionate about. And like the Pied Piper, your tribe will be drawn to you.

Part 1
Summary

The chart below summarizes much of what we've covered so far:

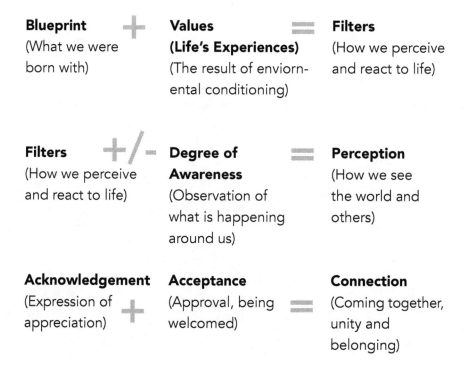

Blueprint + **Values** = **Filters**
(What we were **(Life's Experiences)** (How we perceive
born with) (The result of enviorn- and react to life)
ental conditioning)

Filters +/− **Degree of** = **Perception**
(How we perceive **Awareness** (How we see
and react to life) (Observation of the world and
what is happening others)
around us)

Acknowledgement **Acceptance** **Connection**
(Expression of (Approval, being = (Coming together,
appreciation) + welcomed) unity and
belonging)

PART 2
Your Class

Thirteen

"The way to find meaning in your life is to devote yourself to loving others, devote yourself to your community around you, and devote yourself to creating something that gives you purpose and meaning."
–Mitch Albom

Creating Your Signature Class

A dance, barre, yoga or any other type of physical movement class is comprised of four essential elements:

1. The personality of the teacher and the attitude he/she brings into the class.
2. The primary objective(s) of the class.
3. The content (or medium by which the objectives will be met).
4. The teaching strategies used to meet the objectives.

Separating these elements into categories can help you to

see the big picture. In Part 1 we covered the first essential element thoroughly. We examined our personal approach to the world by identifying our blueprint characteristic, our values and our filters. We became aware of the "window" through which we see, perceive, and respond to others. (Item #1 on the list) The next fifteen chapters address virtually every aspect of each of the next three essential elements of formatting and teaching a successful class. There are many years of experience, trial and error, big mistakes, and wonderful successes outlined in these next pages.

Sharing your passion with others is a gift that not only touches those around you, it affects you as well. It's a self perpetuating cycle: The giver receives and the receiver gives. Having the desire to teach what you love is only the beginning of the process. To create the kind of experience that not only fills your heart, but also the hearts of others, you must acquire an understanding of all the aspects and details that make (assemble) a class. Making the declaration: "I want to be a yoga, barre, or dance teacher!" is the first step of the journey (since all creation begins with a desire and a vision). But if you want to bring a class into being, you must give it a framework.

{ **Your vision requires structure in order to deliver a consistent and organized experience.** }

A few days ago, I received a visit from a young lady who wanted to be considered for a teaching position at dance 101. I was taken a bit by surprise. I walked out of my class and she was waiting for me at the reception (successful interview strategies are discussed in Part 3 and by the way, this is not one of them!). Anyway, she had an idea for a dance fitness class, but she had no teaching experience. She didn't know who her target student group would be (who would enjoy and benefit from her class) and when I asked how she would structure/format her class, what her objectives were, and which teaching strategies she intended to use, she drew a blank.

This is what it looks like to have an idea without a strategy to deliver it. Unfortunately, this is also an example of a mindset that is prevalent among new teachers in today's boutique fitness arena. There is a widespread belief that simply having the desire, knowing how to do something, having an idea or having a certification are all that it takes to teach a successful class. As you read through this book, it will become very clear to you that there is much more involved. If at any point, you begin to feel a bit overwhelmed by all the information, put the book down. Go back over the chapters you have read and let that information sink in deeper before you continue reading.

Dream your dream, but don't stop there. Give it legs! Give it structure!

Fourteen

"How you do anything is how you do everything."
–T. Harv Ecker

Setting Objectives Matters

When I first started teaching, I did not appreciate the importance of setting objectives. I remember just putting together my warm-up routine and choreography, preparing my playlist and showing up for class. I have to admit, it took me a few years to figure out I was missing the mark. But when I did, I added objectives to my classes and began to notice a dramatic increase in my class attendance.

The importance of setting objectives came upon me quite by accident. I was charged with putting together a syllabus for an eight-week beginner jazz course. For the first time in my newly-minted teaching career, I made a list of objectives, mapping out each class over the eight-week period. Until then, all I had taught were on-going, open classes and I hadn't had the experience of working within a time constraint. The experience of teaching those classes felt so . . . clean. I knew what to do. I had a specific destination and every class was a step closer to that. Teaching felt easy, natural, and joyful. Looking back at this experience, I am sure this was when I fell in love with this profession. It made such an impression upon me that I applied this strategy to teaching my other on-going classes. I learned the value of being very clear and intentional about my objectives. I witnessed the effect my clarity had on my students, and I couldn't help but notice a significant reduction in my stress level. I came to realize that when it comes to movement, students don't just want the experience of the class, they also want to know what they are working towards.

Because of my experience in hiring teachers, I know that most of them start off like I did and, unfortunately, some never evolve past a "Just Show Up" mentality. Great teachers are aware of the importance of setting objectives, while other teachers never do, and the ones who don't are unlikely to be successful in the long term. How could they be? How can anyone be successful at anything by just showing up? Certainly, showing up is essential but if we leave it at just that, we're lost. An objective is a destination, and without one in mind, it's the equivalent of just sitting in a parked car or driving in circles.

Author Scott Peck, in his famous book *The Road Less Traveled: A New Psychology of Love, Traditional Values and Spiritual Growth (Simon & Schuster, 2003)*, wrote about the importance of having the right "map" to lead us to where we're going. He devoted an entire chapter to this and essentially proposed three scenarios. I will paraphrase for you. Imagine you live in New York and you want to visit Los Angeles. If you do not have a map, how are you going to get there? Get in your car and just drive? Or let's say you do have a map, but it's to Miami. How likely are you to arrive in Los Angeles? At the end of the day, you need a map to Los Angeles to get to Los Angeles. You might be laughing at how incredibly obvious this is. But honestly, oftentimes I think we tend to overlook the simplest of details. I cannot emphasize enough how important it is for you to set your objectives.

In a competitive urban market, students have many choices. Your students have specific reasons for taking your class and the more focused your class is on its primary objectives, the more successfully you will attract students whose intentions align with those objectives. The content of your class, whether it is yoga, dance, Pilates, barre, etc., should not be your sole objective. Your content is only the medium by which you achieve your objectives. Please make this distinction. Is the primary objective of your class to

" Students don't just want the experience of the class, they also want to know what they are working towards.

provide a meditative experience or a workout? Or both? Or maybe you are teaching terminology and proper execution of the exercises? For restorative benefits? Stress management? To develop greater flexibility? To advance to a higher level of difficulty?

Keep in mind, an excessive number of primary objectives within a single class will likely create an unfocused experience for your students, and it may also overwhelm and frustrate them. Ideally, if your class is an hour long, it should have no more than two primary objectives; three, if the class is more than an hour. The fewer and more focused the primary objectives, the cleaner the experience. Here are some examples: I teach a one-hour class called Dancer's Stretch & Conditioning. This class has, you guessed it, two primary objectives: to develop muscular strength for dance and to develop dance specific flexibility (for leg kicks, splits, and leaps). This class is formatted into two parts, each thirty minutes long. Each part is dedicated to one objective. I also teach a one-hour class called Jazz Funk which has only one primary objective: for students to experience the joy of dance through choreography. My Jazz 101 class is a ninety-minute introductory class which has three primary objectives: to condition the body for dance, to learn how to turn, and how to pick up choreography.

In order to deliver what I consider a clean, focused class, I advise you to set your primary objectives first, and then structure your class around them. Much like a business has its statement of mission or purpose, so should each class you teach. When using your objectives as a compass, it's easier to be creative within the framework you've established because your criteria are clearly defined.

Also consider: Who is your class for? Are you teaching to fitness enthusiasts? Aspiring professionals? To seniors? Boomers? Millennials? Women? Men? Both? Pregnant women? Overweight individuals? Beginners, intermediate or advanced students? Who is your market? *How you teach your content is greatly influenced by who is attending your class.* Your target group must also be included in your primary objectives.

Take a moment to think about the objectives for each class you are teaching (or would like to teach). List them here:

Level:

Target Group:

Length:

Primary Objectives:

1.	
2.	
3.	

As simple as this exercise may appear, it will provide you with very valuable grounding and vision. Without the benefit of this clarity of direction, you will run the risk of being trapped in a "just do, do, do" mentality. Whereas "doing, doing, doing" can appear productive, if there is no intention directing it, it will be just spent energy.

Fifteen

"Excellence is in the details. Give attention to
the details and excellence will come"
–Perry Paxton

Formatting Your Class

Once you have established a clear set of objectives for your class, the next step is to outline the structure of your class. Essentially, a balanced class consists of three parts:

- Part 1: Warm-up
- Part 2: Delivery of Content
- Part 3: Cool Down (Closure)

It is important to assign a specific length of time to each part in accordance with your objectives. Let me explain: The greater the cardio intensity, the longer the warm-up should be (to help prevent injury). The greater level of resistance used to build muscle, the longer the warm-up and cool down should be (muscles need to be prepared to be stressed and must be able to recover afterwards). And the more moderate or low impact the movement, the shorter the warm-up and cool down (less stress on the muscles requires less preparation and recovery).

Another way to look at this is to consider that:

- Your Warm-Up prepares the body.
- Your Content works the body.
- Your Cool Down recovers the body.

These principles apply to all exercise genres and should be used as a guide. Here is a general example:

Sixty-minute class with a single objective

Physicality	Warm-Up	Content	Cool Down
Low impact Light movement	5 minutes	53 minutes	2 minutes
Mid impact Moderate movement	10 minutes	48 minutes	2 minutes
High impact Intense movement	15 minutes	43 minutes	2 minutes

Warm-up, content, cool down. Repeat after me: "Warm-up, content, cool down!" This should be the format of your class—and your new mantra. Once you learn how to create your class using this three-part structure, you'll be amazed at how easy it will be to fulfill your objectives. In addition to being very effective, this framework is also broad enough to afford you the freedom to be creative within it. You can (and should) vary the exercises, content, and stretches after a certain period of time, but the format should always remain the same. This creates consistency in your class experience while also keeping your students' attention. Your regulars will come to expect your class to flow in this order and their bodies will respond positively and naturally to it because of its familiarity (more on this later).

Sixteen

"Begin with the end in mind."
–Dr. Stephen R. Covey

Anatomy of a Warm-Up

A good warm-up before physical activity dilates your blood vessels and ensures that your muscles are well supplied with oxygen. It also boosts your blood flow activating the central nervous system, while enhancing strength, power, and range of motion. Furthermore, it raises your internal body temperature for optimal flexibility and helps minimize stress on the heart. Dynamic stretching is commonly executed during the warm-up segment of a class or prior to any strenuous physical activity. These are stretches that incorporate movement such as trunk rotations, lunges, side bends, moving spinal twists and other low impact, light effort stretches which prepare the joints and muscles for optimal activation. Your warm-up should include dynamic stretches and these stretches should be relevant to the type of activity the body is about to perform.

My daughter Paulina is an avid kickball player. She has played on numerous teams over the past five years and I've enjoyed watching her become a really good player. She competes in an recreational league in Atlanta that holds its games at Piedmont, our central city park. With its gentle rolling hills and verdant game fields, this park provides a beautiful setting to gather with friends, and on a sunny day, playing kickball is a perfect thing to do. I wanted to experience that!

Inspired, I persuaded, cajoled, and pestered my friends into forming a team with me and when we achieved the minimum number required, we registered with the league. Although we were inexperienced players, we were enthusiastic, deciding to call ourselves "Feet Don't Fail Us Now". We had a blast! It was a wonderful summer season and our Sunday afternoon games gave us all something really fun to look forward to. We lost most (if not all) of our games, but winning was never the point. For us it was the experience of being outside and kicking a ball like we used to do as kids.

As team captain (and instigator), I took responsibility for the well-being of my teammates and approached our practices and games in much the same way I would teach a high impact/high-intensity fitness class. Most of us hadn't played in decades and while the majority of us were in fair to good physical condition, I knew from the start that our bodies were not accustomed to the demands of this sport. The nature of the game requires sudden bursts of energy, high-speed directional changes, kicking, catching, and throwing an under-inflated (read: heavy) ball and sliding or diving into the bases. The stress on our bodies would be great and I knew we would likely get injured if we didn't prepare ourselves accordingly. We needed a warm-up—and not just a few stretches here and there. We needed a series of comprehensive dynamic stretches that would address the specific demands this sport would place on our bodies.

In order to design this warm-up, I had to first take into account the ages, physical condition, known physical limitations, and cardio stamina of my teammates. Our youngest player was 30 and our oldest, 60. We had a yogi, a ballroom dancer, a tennis player, an attorney, a photographer, a filmmaker, a therapist, a CPA, two IRS auditors, and a handful of classical dancers. Come to think of it, that's quite a colorful group!

" **As team captain (and instigator), I took responsibility for the well-being of my teammates and approached our practices and games in much the same way I would teach a high impact/ high-intensity fitness class.**

Secondly, I had to factor in which parts of the body would be most vulnerable to trauma. With a little help from Google, I researched the most common kickball injures and found them to be in the hip flexors (Psoas), quadriceps, hamstrings, and knee caps (Patellar tendon). Thirdly, I had to take into consideration the body as a whole.

This is how to create an effective warm-up and what must be considered:

- Who is doing the activity?
- What is involved in the execution of the activity?
- How will the activity impact the body?

Preparing the body for exercise is extremely important, especially if you want to keep your team intact or your students coming back to class. What we do before strenuous activity may accurately predict how long we will be able to engage in that specific activity over the long term.

Back to my kickball warm-up. It became increasingly evident that my two main objectives should be stretching and joint mobility. I began with the arches of the feet and I worked my way up the legs including calves, quads (with extra attention on the Psoas) hamstrings, glutes, then I continued upward through the core to the arms and neck (to avoid pulling, straining or cramping). Then I had us lie on our backs and roll through our ankles, knees, hips, shoulders, and wrists (to stimulate the synovial fluid in the joints for increased mobility). We finished up with a few hip openers (for the sudden directional changes) and a spinal twist (to align and position the spine to better withstand the impact of catching that heavy ball).

Unlike the other teams we played (believe me, I noticed), we were the only group that engaged in a ten to fifteen minute warm-up. I am happy to report we sustained only one pulled quad muscle the entire season and, I must add, it happened to a player who arrived late and did not warm up!

Protect your students. Enable them to keep coming back. Take inventory of what you are asking their bodies to do and put those requests into the context of your audience. If you alter the content of your class, make changes to your warm-up accordingly.

{ **There should always be a direct correlation between content and warm-up in every class you teach.** }

You don't have to have a doctoral degree in anatomical science to figure out what to do. Nor do you need to be able to name every muscle in the body to understand its function. Oftentimes, it will suffice to include a gentler version of some of the exercises you intend to do later on. For example, if your content includes lunges, you can incorporate knee bends into the warm-up to awaken the quadriceps. Does your choreography include pirouettes? Incorporate heel raises into your warm-up. Are you planning on doing arm work with free weights? Do a few of those repetitions without the weights in the warm-up. Stretch class? Warm up the muscle groups you intend to stretch with a light jog and/or extending and contracting those muscles to generate internal body warmth.

To create an effective warm-up, evaluate your content and work your way backwards. Content drives the warm-up. Otherwise, what are you preparing the body for? I think of my warm-up as a conversation with my body in which I am saying: "I am preparing you to do _____." Invest great thought and care in crafting your warm-up. Your students may not realize the degree to which you are taking care of them, but they are very likely to notice improved performance and fewer, or (quite possibly) no injuries.

Seventeen

"Allow your passion to become your purpose,
and it will one day become your profession."
–Gabrielle Bernstein

Great Content

*I*n 2001, business consultant and author, Jim Collins published
*Good to Great: Why Some Companies Make the Leap and
Others Don't (William Collins, 2001),* a management book that
describes how companies transition from being good companies
to being great companies, and how most fail to make the transition.
I picked up this book a few years after opening dance 101 during
my "Holy crap I have a successful business I better figure out what
I'm doing" phase in which I read just about every business book in
print at the time. *Good to Great* will always remain at the top of my
list as one of the most illuminating business books I've ever read. I
remember opening the book to Chapter 1 and reading the words:
"Good is the enemy of great".

Talk about a mic drop. I recall closing the book immediately. It took a good bit of processing to recover from the depth of that statement, as I found myself mentally deconstructing every weekly class I was teaching at the time. Good is the enemy of great, because "good" is . . . well, "good enough".

It gave me pause to think about the aspects of my classes in which I had settled for "good" over "great". Up until that moment, I hadn't stopped the roller coaster I was on to really look at my class content. I thought it was good, but was it the best it could be? And, if not, how could I improve it? This was a major turning point for me as a teacher and studio owner. I wanted to build a great studio. But, what makes a great studio if not great content (classes) and great teachers? And, if I didn't know what great content looked like, how was I going to be able to identify it in the teachers I hired and in the classes they taught? Down the rabbit hole I went in search of excellence and asked myself "What makes for great class content? The answer is "Purpose".

The following table is a visual that shows how all roads lead to purpose. I will explain each one in the next paragraphs.

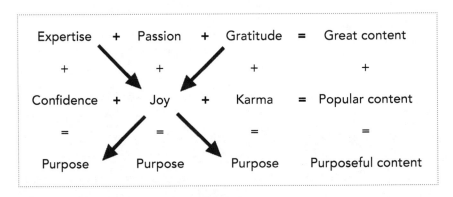

Expertise Leads to Confidence

The knowledge we have equals the information we can share. This requires a realistic look at what we've acquired through training, coaching, experience, study, practice, certifications, etc.

{ **Matching our class level with our knowledge level is a requirement for excellence.** }

Expertise has many levels. However, sometimes our strengths are hidden from view, requiring certain circumstances to bring them into the light. That was me when I started out.

I had been studying dance for ten years when I was invited to teach an eight-week adult beginner jazz workshop for the Center for Lifelong Learning at Emory University in Atlanta. Other than subbing an occasional class for one of my teachers, I had never been asked to teach a class of my own. Thrilled beyond words, I wrote my course description, set the dates, and signed the dotted line. I formatted my class, set objectives, put together my playlist, and created beginner appropriate choreography. The workshop sold out quickly with eighteen students. I was very excited for the opportunity! That is, until the evening before the first class. I had a meltdown.

"What was I thinking? I'm not qualified to teach dance! I never performed professionally. What if my students figure out I'm a fraud?" Harsh, right? I know. It paralyzed me. Convinced I couldn't show up for class, my brain did backflips figuring out how to get out of it: "Maybe I could hand the workshop over to someone who had better qualifications?". . . I worked myself into a panic. It was awful. Fortunately, I was able to talk myself off the ledge with the help of a few of my dance buddies and teachers and the next day I showed up to meet my students. That first class changed the direction of my life. My world spun on its axis. I came alive in that class. Three minutes in and I had forgotten about my anxiety and lack of confidence. All I remember feeling was pure joy. A massive amount of knowledge flowed out of me that I didn't realize I had accumulated. Furthermore, I discovered I could teach to the adult mind because I had learned to dance as an adult.

> ❝ **That is, until the evening before the first class. I had a meltdown.**

I could remember being completely new to dance. I was able to empathize with my students and this enabled me to explain things more effectively, and in a way my students could grasp. By the end of the class, I realized that I was enormously qualified to teach that class, in spite of my lack of experience as a professional dancer. I had discovered my expertise and found my voice as a teacher.

I think it's natural for most of us to experience some degree of anxiety and self-doubt when we first start teaching. We are placing ourselves in front of a group of individuals that have expectations we may or may not be aware of. I've often compared teaching to public speaking. It can be nerve wracking. But, as long as we believe we have something to give, are confident in our training, and we are teaching to the level of our expertise, we can quickly rise above the temporary panic, like I did.

Teach to the level of your expertise. Teach to the level of your physical ability. Be congruent with both of these elements and you will teach with confidence.

Passion Leads to Joy

Passion and joy are typically inclusive emotions. While there are certainly exceptions, for the most part they go hand in hand. In a general sense, most people experience joy when they are engaged in something they feel strongly about, believe in its relevancy and enjoy how it makes them feel about themselves. Passion!

In 2008, James H. Fowler, an American social scientist specializing in social networks, published a highly accredited research paper about the contagiousness of happiness. This study involved 4,739 individuals who were followed from 1983 to 2003. He cites: *"Emotional states can be transferred directly from one individual to another by mimicry and 'emotional contagion' perhaps by the copying of emotionally relevant bodily actions, particularly facial expressions, seen in others. People can 'catch' emotional states they observe in others over time frames ranging from seconds to weeks."*

Think of how this applies to your class, which is one big non-verbal (and verbal) conversation among a group of individuals. Although you may not be exempt from being tagged by one or more individuals who are in a negative emotional state on that particular day, as the leader of the class experience, you set the tone that colors the atmosphere in the room. The strongest emotions prevail. If you are joyful about the experience you are delivering, the power of your joy can be a conduit that conveys a happy feeling to others. Joy is not random for most of us. There's a source behind it and many times it comes from the passion we feel about what we are doing.

How do we communicate joy to our students? With a smile, eye contact, posture, energy level, laughter and . . . gratitude.

Gratitude Leads to Karma

Lauren B. is one of the most celebrated teachers currently on faculty at dance 101. She teaches about twelve classes a week in ballet, barre, stretch, and contemporary dance. Lauren came to us originally as a student about a decade ago, naturally evolving into a teacher over the course of a few years. Besides her warm and friendly nature, enormous talent, and teaching expertise, Lauren is grateful. Every day, without miss, she posts on social media her gratitude for her students and for the opportunity to teach them. Here's a typical post: *"Thank you friends for the most beautiful night of dance! Grateful for Ballet Fit and Inside Out* [her classes], *grateful for the 101, and most of all, grateful for ya'll!"* Here's another: *"Real grateful for a full day of dance. Grateful for dance and the life and clarity it brings. Grateful for a body that moves, grateful for a job I love, and so so grateful for all the amazing folks I get to share it with. Thank ya'll for dancing with me today and all the days!"* Like these, she has posted hundreds of similar ones, all equally genuine and sincere. Lauren's class attendance is consistently high. She is undoubtedly one of the most successful, consistent and longest running teachers on faculty because her students love her energy. Gratitude is a magnet for all good things.

Dr. John D. Moore, in *"Gratitude and Karma"*, identified five specific ways gratitude creates good karma:

- "Gratitude repels negative energy." *(Creating a barrier against the destructive powers of negative thinking)*
- "Gratitude attracts wealth." *(Recognizing the good things we have attract more good things to come)*
- "Gratitude attracts happiness." *(Giving to others causes us to feel good about ourselves)*
- "Gratitude promotes a healthier body." *(An attitude of good health attracts more good health)*
- "Gratitude attracts prosperity." *(A life of security and well-being)*

When we make a conscious effort to focus on the good stuff, we train our minds to look for the good around us and in doing so, it becomes easier to spot positive things which may otherwise pass by undetected. If we define "karma" as what's likely to happen to us, it's easy to understand the importance of gratitude - since what is likely to happen to us has much to do with what we observe and how we feel about it.

I say a prayer of gratitude every evening when I slide into bed. I've been doing this for years. Most of the time, I am at peace with the prayer and it flows easily from me. But on my bad days when I am feeling fearful, frustrated or angry, I have to force myself to utter words of gratitude. No matter how contrived it may feel to express gratitude when things are going wrong, it's a practice that keeps me grounded. I know I have to walk into every class I teach with a clean emotional state. Oftentimes, the pressures and stress of running a business are overwhelming. There are always challenges to face and problems to solve. I can't bring that baggage into class with me. I must be able to tap into my passion for teaching and do it at will, regardless of what's going on in my life. If I were to bring my stress into the classroom, it would impact everyone present and who wants to pay money to experience that?

> **Tap into your gratitude for every one of your blessings, including your passion for teaching, and this will create joy for yourself and others.**

All Roads Lead to Purpose

I hesitate to state anything in the absolute, but I can't think of a single exception to my belief that all great things are made possible when a deep underlying sense of purpose is present. Purpose provides us with clarity about our "why", which is the foundation of "great" content. You may be teaching the same barre exercises everyone else is teaching at your studio, but your purpose in teaching them will set you apart. How strongly do you believe in the transformational effects of your barre workout? How convinced are you that you are contributing to the health and well-being of your students? Are you making it as enjoyable as possible so students return to reap the benefits?

Do you believe that your class will make someone's day better?

Do you believe your class will help distract someone from his or her troubles or sadness? Do you believe your class will help someone live a healthier lifestyle? Do you believe your class will bring people together in friendship? This is the purpose I am referring to.

Author Joey Reiman, in his business book *The Story of Purpose: The Path to Creating a Brighter Brand, a Greater Company, and a Lasting Legacy* (*John Wiley & Sons, 2012*), wrote: *"I have consistently found that the best companies are the ones that want to make the world more successful. Purpose driven organizations create more good in the world, which begets greater profit, which allows them to then create even more*

> **Purpose provides us with clarity about our "why", which is the foundation of "great" content.**

good. It's a virtuous, never-ending circle." Although written in the context of business, we can extrapolate this concept to any service we provide, whether we're paid to do it or not. If we run everything we do through the filter of "Will this contribute to making the world a better place?", we would live with a higher purpose. Great content is purposeful content.

Eighteen

"The first five minutes sets the tone, but it is the last five minutes they will remember"
–Ofelia de La Valette

Cool Down and Closure

Warming up and cooling down are important parts of every exercise class. They help transition the body from a resting state to an active state and back to resting. A gradual increase in physical intensity and a subsequent gradual decrease in activity helps prevent injury and can ease soreness among your students.

One of the most important functions of the post-exercise cool down is to prevent dizziness. Strenuous exercise causes the blood vessels in the legs to expand, bringing more blood into the legs and feet. When we stop exercising suddenly without taking time to cool down, our heart rate slows abruptly and the blood can be pooled into our lower body, causing dizziness and even fainting.

The cool down has psychological benefits as well. It can be a celebratory moment in a class in which students may revel in a deep sense of accomplishment. Another benefit is to restore a "sense of normalcy" to the body enabling a return to other daily activities.

For me, I've always viewed the cool down period as a potentially productive time to optimally work warm muscles for greater flexibility. It is also a great opportunity to practice relaxation techniques, capitalizing on the muscle fatigue that follows cardio intense movement and/or strength training. Use your cool down productively!

While you're at it, create a signature close—something specific to your personality. You can do this with a particular piece of music you always play, or a particular choreographed sequence of movement. Music can be a powerful anchor that triggers a particular state of mind. Use this to your advantage. Give some thought to how you wish to send your students back into their day. Energized and upbeat? Choose a song with an uplifting message. Relaxed and at peace? Play a soothing instrumental.

Whatever you do, don't just abruptly end your class, turn off your music, collect your things and leave! Let your students know the cool down is coming and that the class will be over soon. If it's possible for you to end the class with a few minutes remaining in the hour, leave the music on (at a lower volume) and walk around your class to interact with your students. I've seen many popular teachers do this. It's a classy send off. You greeted everyone at the beginning of the class, but some may have arrived late. This gives you a wonderful opportunity to show gratitude by acknowledging who is present. Plus you have just shared an experience. Your students will feel connected to you and may appreciate the opportunity to ask you a question or simply thank you for the class.

This is the beauty of a well planned cool down and closure. The work in class has been completed and the objectives have been fulfilled. The finishing touch is the human element: gratitude and connection.

Nineteen

"The body becomes what the body does."
–Ofelia de La Valette

Stretching to Achieve
Greater Flexibility

*J*ust as there are different levels of flexibility, there are also different methods of stretching. Each method accomplishes different objectives. To achieve a greater level of flexibility with an expanded range of motion, the three most popular methods are:

- Static Active
- Static Passive
- Isometric

Let's look at each one.

Static Active stretches build muscular strength while also elongating the muscles being worked. A targeted muscle is placed into a position by the force of the contraction of an opposing muscle.

A great example of this would be a leg lift where you can stretch the back of the leg while simultaneously strengthening the front of the hip that is lifting the leg. This process used alone is not as effective at achieving greater flexibility as when it is combined with static passive stretching. However, it may have a place in your class if your objective is geared more toward conditioning with only a mild stretch component. Static active stretching is commonly found in today's popular barre workouts.

Static Passive stretching occurs when muscles are held in an extended position for a period of time. Commonly thought of as a "deep" stretch, static passive stretching is a characteristic of yoga where a muscle is stretched to its furthest point then held there for a number of breaths. This type of stretching uses body weight under the force of gravity to pull on a targeted muscle for at least twenty seconds.

Isometric is a type of static stretching which involves the resistance of muscle groups through isometric contractions (tensing) of the stretched muscles. Believed to be the most effective way to develop greater flexibility, this method can employ the use of manual resistance as well as bands and straps. Often a partner is engaged to assist in the application of resistance or a free weight is placed on the muscle being contracted (stretched). In dance, we frequently use the floor, the barre or a wall as resistance. Isometric exercises are typically sustained for seven to fifteen seconds at a time. This type of stretching is considered to be quite aggressive (hence its effectiveness) and therefore should not be done on a daily basis. Some experts recommend a good thirty-six-hour rest period between isometric workouts. Please keep this in mind (more for yourself than your students) if you are teaching multiple classes per week.

One reason ballet training produces such flexible dancers is because it incorporates all three of these methods of static stretching.

Ballet barre work is mostly static active where muscles are engaged while working to be lengthened. Additionally, ballet training includes static passive stretching in which dancers will "sit" in stretches or use the barre to stabilize the body in a stretch for several minutes at a time. In floor barre, where typical barre exercises are done laying down, dancers use the floor for isometric resistance and to maintain a straighter spine.

Now let's take a look at the physiology of these methods. When we think of stretching we tend to focus on muscles, but in reality, we engage our ligaments, tendons, and fascia as well!

Ligaments are tight, rubbery collagenous tissues that connect bone to bone. Tendons connect muscles to bone. To acquire greater flexibility, our muscles, ligaments, and tendons must be elongated to reach beyond whatever limitation they've developed in adaptation to the physical mechanics of our everyday lives. Static and isometric stretches, if held long enough, can reach deep into the ligaments, tendons, muscle, and engage fascia. Whereas all these connective tissues and muscles must be lengthened to achieve a greater level of flexibility, great care must be taken to avoid injury.

{ **The best way to safely extend beyond the body's present capability is to understand how it responds to an unfamiliar or infrequent stretch.** }

As you initiate a stretch, your muscles reflexively tense up; this is the body's way of protecting itself from injury. If the stretch is held for about fifteen to twenty seconds, the muscle relaxes and you are more likely able to access the ligament and joint (where flexibility originates). Once the muscle has relaxed it can be safely contracted and/or stretched. Muscles are wrapped in fascia, a very strong connective tissue. Fascia behaves much like a ligament in that it will release during a sustained stretch after a specific period of time. For the connective tissue to release, a stretch should be held statically for (at least) thirty seconds and up to five minutes.

There is another element at work when we engage in active or passive stretching. I have found no scientific data to support this theory but I believe the mind and body need to be coaxed to release into a stretch. Throughout my own personal journey to become more flexible as well as the anecdotal data I've collected from my students over the years, I couldn't be more convinced that we have not one, but two minds: One in our brain and one in our body. Many times they argue, disagree and fight one another! In designing my Dancer's Stretch, a class I've been teaching for more than twenty years, I incorporated a "dialog" between the "brain mind" and the "body mind" to create a sense of safety as we progress from one stretch to another. We start off with an easy stretch; a light nudge. After a few repetitions, we progress to a stronger nudge and from there each stretch gradually becomes more intense. Keep in mind that the slower the body eases into a stretch, the greater the likelihood the connective tissue and muscles will release. Ultimately, I see my students successfully doing rather aggressive stretches using this method.

If achieving greater flexibility is one of your class objectives, consider a combination of static passive, static active, and isometric stretching. Once you've designed your stretch, organize the sequences in a progressive presentation that gradually increases in intensity. Remind your students that in order to break boundaries, the body must become familiar with your stretch sequences (to facilitate the body's acceptance of these stretches). It is through repetition and consistency that the body experiences physical benefits. Rest between stretch classes is also important as the body needs time to heal. In fact, it is in the healing process that the effects of stretching stick.

At the end of the day, the body becomes what the body does. If we spend forty hours a week sitting at a desk, hunched over a computer screen, our muscles, tendons, and ligaments adapt to this position. If we are constantly slumped over with internally rotated shoulders, the ligaments in the front of the shoulder actually shorten since they are chronically held in that position. Ligaments can become shortened due to trauma or faulty posture, but they can also become lengthened using specific types of exercises that include a regular regimen of static stretching. The process of "un-doing" the mechanical effects our lifestyles have imprinted upon us requires time and patience. But it is very possible.

I often use myself as an example to my students. I came to dance late in life. I was extremely inflexible and had very bad posture. Over time and study, I was able to overcome these aspects of my physical being, develop great flexibility, and acquire skills that would later enable me to teach dance professionally after only ten years of study at age forty-four. It is never too late to become proficient in any physical endeavor. If your students desire greater flexibility, they can achieve it. Design a plan and implement a strategy toward that end. Then "sit back" and watch your students transform.

> ❝❝ **It is through repetition and consistency that the body experiences physical benefits.**

Twenty

"You never know how strong you are until being
strong is your only choice"
–Bob Marley

Reaching Deep (On Those Days...)

*I*t was springtime in Atlanta in 2006, on a Monday evening. I
was about midway through my Dancer's Stretch class when
I felt a wave of discomfort come over me. I didn't know what was
wrong. I had just finished a particularly strenuous set of abdominal
exercises and felt that maybe my muscles had cramped up. Reaching
deep to find my resolve, I hid my discomfort and made it through
the rest of the class. Afterwards, I informed the front desk that I was
not feeling well and I headed home. I remember that fifteen-minute
drive. By the time I got into my car, the pain in my core was almost
unbearable. Driving home clutching my stomach, I arrived safely and
headed upstairs, grabbed my trusty heating pad and curled up in
bed (in a fetal position) with the pad on its highest setting. It was

8:30 p.m. Instead of feeling better, the pain became progressively worse and around midnight I asked my husband to drive me to the emergency room.

By the time we arrived at the ER, the pain was so intense, I could barely speak. Upon examination, the attending physician ordered a series of blood and urine tests and gave me some terrible tasting liquid to drink. A few hours later I was placed in a CT scanner. The results came back quickly: I had a ruptured appendix. At 5 a.m., I was prepped and wheeled into emergency surgery. I called my mother as I lay on the gurney being rolled into the operating room. My appendix was coming out and in a hurry!

Looking back, it really amazes me how much power our minds have over our bodies. I was not going to stop my class because I didn't feel well. How could I disappoint the twenty-five or so people who were in the class with me? Over a stomach cramp? Nope, not doing that! Teaching while feeling unwell is something all fitness teachers experience at some time or another. When it happens, we push through.

I'm not suggesting you teach with a ruptured appendix. Honestly, if I had known that's what had happened to me, I would have ended my class immediately and headed directly to the emergency room. What I am suggesting is that you develop a strategy or strategies to help you get through a challenging day. Waiting for it to happen and then figuring out how to cope is not a good strategy. Don't let it take you by surprise!

You will have days in which you are distracted. Something may be weighing on your mind: a worry, an upset, anxiety, physical discomfort, fatigue, muscle soreness, heartache, grief, etc. There are any number of things that can pull your concentration out of the present and into the past or future. Or maybe it's such extreme physical discomfort that your mind and body are screaming. It happens to all of us and it's a particular challenge for those of us whose job is physical and requires us to be upbeat for others. These are the hard days, and because we will have them, it's necessary to have a strategy to help us cope and get through the hour without transferring our state of mind to those in our classes.

The strategy I typically use involves distraction and gratitude. To distract myself, I will focus on the music. Often, I'll sing along in my head to drown out the voice inside that may be on a rant. Or, I may add a few new exercises or movements that challenge me, so I am forced to focus on my body. On some occasions, I will add new music to my playlist that I'm not terribly familiar with. This forces me to concentrate intensely on what I'm doing to make sure I sync my movement and exercises up with the new music. I will also focus outward onto my students— more so than usual—by stepping away from the center of the room and moving closer to each one, alternating from one person to the other. Or, I will introduce an exercise many are already familiar with and step away from demonstrating to watch and correct form. This strategy is most effective when I'm in my head about something that is bothering me.

> **Any strategy that empowers you to overcome physical discomfort or emotional turmoil for an hour, can potentially get you through even bigger things in life.**

But by far, the most effective strategy for me is the expression of gratitude. This is how I got through my stretch class on the day my appendix decided to call it quits. I kept telling myself that I was doing what I love, that I'd deal with the pain afterward, and it was going to be fine. And it was! Eventually.

When I'm in class and the voice in my mind says "I don't want to do this right now", I will typically launch into a lecture to myself. I remind myself that the day will come when I can no longer do this. I think about how much I love to teach and how lucky I am to be doing it. I tell myself: "Yes, I am uncomfortable, but it will pass and tomorrow will be better." I recall the many years of training that have prepared me to be able to teach for a living and how important it is for me to have this in my life. I think about all the people in the class that have moved mountains to spend an hour with me and how, because of my "purpose", I am contributing to their lives, their bodies, their minds, and also helping them through *their* bad days. These are all "big picture" thoughts that help me put everything I am feeling into perspective and push through momentary discomfort. Difficult days are a given. We all have them. You will have them!

> "I remind myself that the day will come when I can no longer do this. I think about how much I love to teach and how lucky I am to be doing it.

Another strategy that works for me is to reframe these experiences as a guaranteed aspect of life, making it easier for me to accept them. If we can see the value of our hardship, we benefit. As silly as it may sound, teaching a packed out class with a ruptured appendix taught me something very important about my strength and resolve. I emerged from that experience with renewed confidence in myself. If I could do that, I could do anything. It made me feel strong.

Accept that you will have uncomfortable days and in doing so, believe that you will benefit from having them—in one way or another. Develop a coping strategy to get you through and make a mental note of it. Any strategy that empowers you to overcome physical discomfort or emotional turmoil for an hour, can potentially get you through even bigger things in life.

It may take some trial and error on your part and you may

not know at this point how to even begin to design your strategy. My suggestion is that you take what sounds useful from my strategy and begin there. Over time you'll figure out exactly what you need to get you through and you'll be ready when the day comes.

Let me end on a positive note here. Challenging days are few and far between. I've never counted but my best guess is that I might have one every few months—if that. And on the occasions when I am having a difficult time in my personal life (I've been through a number of these), what I've found is that at some point in my grief or journey through despair, my mindset flips from having to reach deep to teach my classes, to experience the emotional healing teaching plays in my recovery.

Twenty-one

"Be the kind of teacher that believes in your
students before they start believing in themselves."
–Justin Tarte

Teaching Movement
to the Unfamiliar Mind

*T*his chapter is devoted to those of you who wish to teach any
form of beginner dance or dance fitness. For the purposes
of this chapter, "dance" refers to any type of creative movement that
is attached to, or built upon, a musical phrase and falls into one
(or more) of the following categories: *Pedestrian, Technical, and
Isolated Movement.*

"**Pedestrian**" is a term used to describe movement that
is natural to the body. This type of movement is achievable by
almost anyone who is physically capable of participating in any
type of group fitness. Dance fitness, Zumba, NIA, Gabriele Roth's
5Rhythms, Jazzercise and Hip Hop, as well as certain types of modern

dance are some examples of pedestrian movement.

"**Technical**" describes movement that is made possible by means of a structured training program that expands the body's natural ability to move beyond its innate limitations. It is characterized by precision of movement using the position of arms, feet and body designed to enable the body to move with agility, control, lightness and speed. Ballet and tap are great examples of this.

"**Isolated**" movement trains specific areas of the body to move in precise ways while the remainder of the body is relatively still. Belly dance and Pop 'n Lock (hip hop) are good examples of this. "Isolation" is also a form of technical dance because it requires training.

Some dance forms incorporate all three categories. Jazz, modern, lyrical, contemporary and musical theater, are some examples. These dance genres have a technical foundation in ballet, upon which pedestrian and isolated movements are typically layered.

Choreography is the art or practice of designing sequences of movement that are inspired by music and expressed using the six or four-count musical phrases upon which a musical composition is created. Most commercial pop music is built upon a four-count phrase. Less common is the six-count phrase which is typically found in the waltz and West Coast Swing. A count is the measurement of a beat.

The choreography you create for your class will most typically be built upon the count measures of the beat in the music you are using. However, some choreographers, particularly in hip hop, lyrical and contemporary, may create movement that follows the story line (lyrics) in a song. How you create your movement is how you should expect to teach it. Teaching "on the count" will require you to present your work by assigning a specific move to a specific number count. Teaching to the story line will require you to teach the lyrics of the song while you demonstrate the movement associated with each phrase.

Regardless of which genre of dance you are teaching, or whether your choreography was created on counts or lyrics, if your class consists of students who are new to the experience, it's very helpful to understand how the student-mind processes new information. There are certain strategies you can implement that will more effectively present your material in a way in which your students can assimilate. To better understand these strategies, let's take a look at how the unfamiliar mind and body respond to movement.

- Response 1: The mind speeds up its cognitive processes.
- Response 2: The body tightens up.
- Response 3: Memory diminishes.
- Response 4: Mental chatter blocks incoming data.

Disclaimer: While "How the Mind Processes New Information" is a vast enough topic to fill an entire book in which empirical evidence can be presented in support of the latest theories, what I am offering to you here is a summary of what I've learned over the past twenty-five years of teaching.

These four responses may or may not unfold in this precise order. In fact, I have strong evidence to suspect they may actually manifest concurrently. What's important is that you are aware of them, so you can recognize the ones you can address or bypass and accept the ones you cannot. These responses will sabotage the process of learning in relationship to the degree of intensity of each response. That means, the greater the experience of the intensity, the lower the level of absorption and vice versa.

If your message (what you are teaching) is not getting through these common barrier responses, your students may become frustrated and subsequently be discouraged from returning. This is a dynamic that's present at all levels of instruction; however, it is strongest at the introductory and beginner levels.

As students progress, they amass a growing inventory of dance moves, diminishing the quantity of new and unfamiliar material they experience in class. Nonetheless, when new information is presented, even the most advanced student may engage in any or all of these responses, albeit less intensely than a beginner.

- **Response 1: The mind speeds up its cognitive processes.**
If you were to demonstrate a complete eight-count phrase to newly minted students, the first time they see it, they may only remember the first and possibly one other count. The remaining six counts will have whizzed past their conscious mind. The most effective way to bypass this response is to slow down the speed at which you present your movement and to present your movement in smaller increments. If the mind can only process two of the eight counts, start there. Demonstrate the first two counts of movement and repeat these two moves until you are satisfied that the information has been received. Now add the second two new counts to the first and repeat the four counts. Continue this process of adding two new counts at a time until those counts are mastered, then add them to what has already been learned. Eventually, you will build a nice combination (choreography) and will have achieved your goal for the class. The only difference is that you've done it in smaller pieces than how it is typically done.

> **This strategy goes completely against the grain of how dance has been taught for centuries.**

During my tenure as a dance student, I never experienced a teacher present choreography two counts at a time. It was always presented in complete four or eight count phrases. I soon came to learn that one of the differences between a beginner and an advanced level dance class was the number of times the eight-count phrase was repeated before the students were expected to learn it. In a beginner class, the phrase may be demonstrated six to eight times while in an advanced class, it might be shown three to four times. Professional level dancers are expected to learn choreography with only two demonstrations, maybe three. Granted, picking up choreography quickly and in larger pieces is a skill that comes with time and practice. To this day, most technical dance classes continue to present choreography in eight-count phrasing.

When I began teaching beginners, my strategy of presenting two counts at a time was not something I had learned to do. It was what my logical mind told me to do, based upon my own early struggles to capture and retain movement. An eight-count phrase can be anywhere from eight to eighteen different body positions or movements (depending on how many syncopated counts are in the phrase). That is a lot of information! In summary: To bypass the speeding up of the unfamiliar mind, present smaller pieces and engage in lots of repetition. Once your beginner class gels and your students become familiar with your choreographic style, you can add choreography in larger increments. This will happen organically over time.

• Response 2: The body tightens up.

I have witnessed this on countless occasions. I believe the body is physiologically programmed to protect itself and when we attempt to move our muscles in unfamiliar ways, the body responds by tightening up. This is the body's self-defense mechanism kicking into gear. This may explain why we tend to look and feel awkward when we are attempting to learn new movement. It's an interesting conversation between the mind and body—which is actually more like an argument in reality. The mind issues a command: "Do this!" And the body responds: "No, we might get hurt." As silly as this may sound, this is my layman's explanation of this phenomenon. Use repetition. The more the body repeats a movement, the less threatened it will perceive the movement to be. The unfamiliar becomes familiar. The body becomes what the body does with regularity. Your new students may have an uncooperative body on their hands, and the only way you will calm their innate self-defense mechanism is through repetition.

- **Response 3: Memory diminishes.**

You've just finished an hour-long dance class in which your students learned and practiced a choreographic combination for as much as forty-five minutes. By the time they get home and try showing it to someone (as in: "Look what we did in class today!"), your student discovers they can't remember all of it. Maybe they only remember a few eight counts—if even that. How is this possible?

A common challenge beginner dancers face is remembering choreography. Specifically, in a class setting, the challenge is remembering what comes next. As long as the teacher is dancing alongside, students can remember. But the moment the teacher steps away to watch, students forget what to do, or lose the timing of the counts or only remember certain parts of the combination. Some will start off strong then freeze a few counts in. It's not that your students aren't paying attention. They just can't remember.

Fortunately, a diminished capacity to remember is something that eventually goes away with time. But in the meantime, it's a very real dynamic you must be aware of. There is no quick fix, it takes practice and, you guessed it, repetition. One helpful strategy you can employ to overcome this is to repeat your choreographic combinations from class to class. In my experience, it takes about four consecutive classes for beginners to master a combination. But be careful, more is not necessarily better. By the sixth consecutive repetition of a combination, it may become stale. By the seventh time, your students may want to dance to something new.

Most dance fitness formatted classes present specific choreography created for a particular song. Each time that song is played, the class engages in that specific choreography. As long as the class playlist varies from one class to the next, you can repeat combinations many more than seven times—mainly because it's only one of maybe ten songs on your playlist. But if your class is formatted more like a traditional dance class, your combination is the entire class and for forty-five minutes you might be playing the same song. Although it is through the use of repetition that you will overcome your students' diminished memory, be tuned into the non-verbal cues your students are sending you. They will let you know when it may be time to move on to a new song and new choreography.

- **Response 4: Mental chatter blocks incoming data.**
This happens to everyone. There's not much a teacher can do about this, other than simply be aware. Whether it's a new student with internal conversations raging on: "I can't do this, it's too fast, I'm in over my head, everyone is better than me, I feel stupid . . . " etc., or it's a seasoned student who's mind is occupied by something going on in his or her life at that moment, when our inner voice is on a rant, incoming environmental data gets blocked.

 Personally, I think it is virtually impossible to learn something new when we are not able to concentrate and it can be very frustrating to try.

When you notice students are distracted, the best course of action is to ease back. Don't push them. Give them the space to work things out. Be compassionate about their inner tug of war and their struggle to focus outwardly when their thoughts are pulling them inward. Give them an occasional smile and if you've gotten to know them personally, you can inquire privately after class if you feel compelled to do so.

There really is no way to bypass this response. The only course of action I can recommend is to accept and be aware that your students are experiencing this mental chatter with varying intensity. Any effort a teacher might put into trying to help a student "snap out of it" may be futile in that specific moment. A compassionate conversation after class may have some effect. But honestly, there are times in our lives when we should speak and others when we should remain silent. By being observant and highly connected, teachers will develop a sense for what to do when the time comes.

In summary, when teaching to the unfamiliar mind, it is important to reduce the number of counts presented together and engage in more repetition before introducing new movements. Also, offering words of encouragement may help students to feel accepted and appreciated.

Twenty-two

"The art of teaching is the art of assisting discovery."
–Mark Van Doren

Top Nine Teaching Methods

*T*here are nine universal teaching methods used to teach movement. They are:

- Demonstration
- Mimicry (follow along)
- Correction
- Repetition
- Drills
- Consistency (in how the material is presented)
- Breaking boundaries
- Modifications
- Imagery

These methods can be applied to different types of movement, from Pilates to Spinning, barre, yoga, boot camp, dance fitness, ballet, etc., in one or multiple combinations depending on the objective of the training. For instance, let's say the objective is competition (of any kind); we would not apply Mimicry and Modifications but would apply Demonstration, Correction, Repetition, Drills, Consistency, Breaking Boundaries and Imagery. For aspiring professional dancers, omit Modifications and keep the rest. For yoga, remove Drills and Repetition (and maybe Mimicry—depending on the teacher). For dance fitness, remove Demonstration, Correction, Drills, Breaking Boundaries and Modifications but use Mimicry, Repetition and Consistency. Determining the appropriate methods for your classes is very easy once you have a clear understanding of each one.

• Demonstration

Demonstration is used to present a sequence of exercises or movement that a teacher is asking students to do, before they are expected to do them.

• Mimicry

Mimicry or "follow along" is typically seen in classes where the teacher is leading the movement. Students will look to the teacher for cues to indicate changes in direction or exercises. The teacher is an active participant in the class. Mimicry is a great strategy for workout classes because the teacher will typically move at a faster pace than students may otherwise choose. Dance fitness, Jazzercise and Zumba instructors use mimicry to keep their classes going for extended periods of time. If calorie burn and cardio health are your objectives, this is how to do it!

• Correction

Correction is used to teach proper placement and execution of the material typically seen in yoga, body sculpting, Pilates, weight lifting and ballet, but also in other forms of technical dance such as jazz, contemporary, lyrical and tap. Correction is necessary not only to train muscles for precise movement but also to prevent over exertion and injury. Correction will also accelerate progress as the body is being coerced into an activity that doesn't come naturally. This requires the teacher to observe her students versus being an active participant in the class at any given time.

• Repetition

Repetition is used to stimulate memory. Whether it's a particular dance step or the proper way to lift a 5 lb weight, it is through repetition that the mind and body learn. In dance fitness classes, repetition is used to remember choreography. In yoga and stretch classes, repetition helps the body to relax into familiar poses, achieving a greater level of flexibility and strength. Repetition can also build endurance and cardio health. Executing a specific movement repeatedly and in rapid succession will elevate the heart rate. Use repetition if your class is cardio in nature. Beginner dance students also benefit from the use of repetition since many of the dance moves they are learning are new to them. Repetition strengthens the mind-body connection enabling students to develop a greater degree of muscular coordination.

• Drills

Drills are most commonly seen in competitive sports and dance. Essentially, any physical activity which requires a specific set of skills will employ the use of drills. These are repetitive exercises that work specific muscle groups necessary for the purpose of mastering specific tasks. Drills are very effective because of their repetitive nature. If there are specific moves or exercises that need to be mastered in your class, devise a series of drills to help your students master them.

In a dance fitness or hip hop class, you can incorporate drills into your warm-up. This not only adds to the productivity of the warm-up, but also prepares the muscles for movement and enhances the practice of specific skills.

• Consistency

Consistency refers to how material is presented. In technical dance, there is only one correct way of executing a particular turn or leap. In any specific yoga discipline, there is only one correct way of positioning the body for a pose (unless a modification is given). Where there is uniformity, there must be consistency in the way the form is taught. This means the method used to teach the move should be repeated with little to no variation. In my beginner jazz class, I teach single pirouettes. I always say the same things, demonstrate the same mechanics, discuss the same physiology, and employ the same practice drills. I've watched my students thrive with this method, some becoming really fantastic turners. At times I think I sound like a broken record, but if you've got a system that works, be consistent with it.

• Breaking Boundaries

Breaking Boundaries is a teaching method whereby a teacher will nudge a student beyond a current physical limitation, whether it means extending the leg an inch higher, or encouraging one more rotation in a turn. It may mean suggesting a 3 lb instead of a 1 lb hand weight, or adding ten more crunches to the customary set. Fitness is a journey. There is no end to how strong, flexible, graceful or skillful anyone can become. Pushing past limitations is part of any evolutionary and transformational journey. As teachers we must be aware of where our students are on this journey and rely on our instincts to know when to nudge them towards greater accomplishment. Stagnation leads nowhere. There's no growth in comfort. If you notice your students becoming comfortable, it may be time to press on, but just a tad! Be careful not to make any dramatic changes to the class as a whole. If you are teaching a beginner class, it must remain beginner.

• Modifications

A modification is an alteration made to an exercise for the purpose of accommodating a particular physical limitation. They are commonly used in yoga where the employment of blocks and straps can help achieve proper form. Modification can be a great teaching tool— if used temporarily. With equal pros and cons, modifications can help students propel forward, but they can also hold them back. How the modifications are used is the determining factor. Unless a student has a long term limitation (injury, joint replacement) or attends so sporadically that progress is not possible, modifications should not be given over the long term. The end goal should be to wean students off them, (although there isn't much you can do if students have embraced their modifications on a more permanent basis). Not everyone has a "breaking boundaries" mindset. Some are content to simply engage in some sort of exercise. Trust your instincts when applying modifications. If you feel the student has potential and is ambitious, work with him or her to overcome the modification (see "Breaking Boundaries" above) with gradual adjustments until the exercise, pose or stretch is executed in its fullest expression.

• Imagery

Using imagery is a teaching method that engages the mind in visual pursuit of an objective. In dance, we often see it used to explain the nuances in the expression of choreography or to evoke a feeling about a musical composition. This will add emotional depth to the movement. Many choreographers use imagery to inspire beautiful performances from their dancers. Many teachers do the same to inspire meaningful performances from their students. Imagery is often used in ballet, contemporary, lyrical, modern as well as any type of movement that tells a story.

Imagery is also used to help draw awareness into the body. We see this most commonly used in the Franklin and Feldenkrais Methods. Although different in their approaches, these disciplines create a new conversation between the mind and the body through the use of mental imagery (as well as anatomical knowledge). Students are asked to visualize their body (skeleton, joints and muscles) moving a certain way prior to engaging in the actual exercise. You'd be surprised how effective these methodologies are!

Imagery is also used by many fitness instructors; typically at the high point of muscle burn or fatigue. It always helps to have a visual of our end goal: "Six weeks to bikini season! Ten more reps! Let's GOOOOO!!!"

Whether used to evoke a feeling, visualizing the body moving in a particular way or as a motivator to keep going, imagery can be a very powerful teaching tool and a great complement to the other eight methods.

Which of the above teaching methods apply to your content? List them here:

1.	4.	7.
2.	5.	8.
3.	6.	9.

Twenty-three

"The art of communication is the language of leadership."
–James Humes

The Art of Cueing

One of the biggest challenges in teaching dance and instructional fitness is communicating with students over the intrusiveness of very loud music. To keep students stimulated and motivated in these classes, music is typically played at a high volume. Some boutique fitness studios go so far as to offer ear plugs to students—which is well intended—but also prevents students from hearing the teacher as well. Some studios place decibel meters next to the sound equipment in hopes teachers will adjust their volume to safe levels. Offering instruction in such a noisy setting requires a skillful mix of cues using voice, hand and body gestures. Let me break it down for you.

• Talking Over the Music

Cueing is how a teacher communicates with her students when the music is playing. Relying solely on your voice to prompt changes may work if you've got a microphone or a head piece. Otherwise, your cueing must work in harmony with your music, not in competition with it. Too much talking over the music can be overwhelming and even annoying to students. Too little talking can also be problematic if students are not familiar with the class content. If your music has lyrics, even if played at a lower volume, avoid talking over them. Wait until there's a pause between the lyrics or an instrumental section between vocals to give a verbal cue.

• Delivering Timely Cues

Cues that are untimely or difficult to understand can severely compromise the enjoyment of any class. A cue given too late can result in knocking students off count. Giving no cues at all can be frustrating for your students, unless they already know what comes next. How well a class flows from one movement to another is determined by the teacher's ability to clearly cue changes ahead of time.

When a teacher effectively cues, those present can relax. Good cues remove the worry many students experience about falling behind because they are unsure of what comes next. Students will feel secure, knowing the teacher will guide them. The result is a seamless class experience that can be quite glorious.

• Let Your Voice Be Heard!

A teacher's cue must be heard. You cannot be shy about it. Project your voice! This does not mean you need to shout at the top of your lungs. This can be irritating! Students will tense up if a teacher is screaming. Most people are conditioned to react this way to screaming in general. Projecting your voice does not mean simply adding volume; projecting involves lowering your voice a pitch or two and vocalizing from the diaphragm. If your voice cannot be heard, it is worse than not giving any cues at all. When your students think they hear you give a cue, but are not sure because your cues are barely audible, students will strain to hear you and this makes for an unpleasant experience for them.

• Anticipation and Identification

An effective cue requires two actions on your part:

1. You must anticipate what comes next.
2. You must give the cue prior to the change (not during and certainly not afterwards!).

This requires you to be at least one step ahead of what is happening in the moment. For this reason, it is important that your warm-up, content and cool down are mapped out. You can make spontaneous alterations and be creative, but only within an established framework. If you don't know what's coming, you can't expect to be able to communicate what's ahead! Furthermore, it is very helpful to give a verbal or visual indication that a change is about to take place. Use your voice in one to two syllable commands for example: up, down, right, left, around, right/left foot, right/left arm, roll down, plié, point, flex, beat, push-ups! Crunches! Yoga can be easier to cue since each pose has a name. Other workouts have their own terminology as well, e.g., burpees, plank jacks, jump squats, lunges, tuck, hold, bend stretch, pulse, etc. Using your genre's terminology is a great way to cue. Even if the word is not understood at first, students will learn to associate the word with the movement.

• Verbal Cues, Gestures, or Both?

Be cognizant of whether or not your students can see you and if not, for how long they will not have you in view. If you have them in a forward bend in which they are facing the back of the room and you are in the front, students will only have the sound of your voice to indicate a change is coming. This will cause students to look up or look at you to see what's going on.

When you are in full view of your students, you are not solely dependent on your voice. Hand gestures are great to use in this scenario and have the added benefit of being independent of the music. You don't have to wait until a pause in the song to voice a cue. Hand gestures, by virtue of being silent, can be delivered at any time regardless of the music. Going to the left? Point to the left, and then go there. Stepping back on the right leg? Tap the leg with your right hand and point to the back. Working a specific muscle group? Point to it or tap it with your hand. Essentially what you're doing is using hand gestures to draw your students' attention to a particular area of the body, or to remind them of the next step and in which direction you want them to go.

In Chapter 24, The Final Touch: Visual, Auditory and Kinesthetic, we will discuss the simultaneous engagement of three of our five senses during communication and how this improves the assimilation of our message. If your students can see you (Visual) and hear you (Auditory), you have two of the three communication faculties (and two of the five senses) stacked in your favor. When you use your voice and hand gestures simultaneously, you greatly reduce the likelihood of misunderstanding.

• The Art of Cueing Is in the Timing

This all sounds fairly straightforward, so, what's the big deal? Why do some consider great cueing to be an art? The answer lies in the timing of the cue. A class in which music is played (at high volume) requires a greater level of cohesiveness between movement and the beats in a song. In other words, unless your music is irrelevant background sound, played at a low volume and has no motivating function, your movement, as well as your cues, must be on the count, otherwise your movement will feel disjointed. All changes should occur at the top of the eight-count drop and one syllable cues should be called out on the seventh count. Two and three syllable cues should begin sooner. The cue must be delivered by the seventh count.

This requires a working understanding of how music is structured, a topic we'll examine in Chapter 26: Deconstructing Your Music to Attach Movement. Teachers must be able to identify the top of the eight-count and understand the musical framework of each song they use in class. Furthermore, all movement (and exercises) should be paired with this framework. For example, if the refrain in a song is six 8-counts, that's three 8-counts of movement on each side of the body. Three 8-counts equals twenty-four total counts. Cues should be delivered at count twenty-three (or on the twenty-third repetition of the exercise) to change to the other side, and at count forty-seven to change to the next move ahead. This creates balance and harmony with your soundtrack.

• A Cue Is Not Meant to Be Instructional

A cue is an advanced notice of what's next. It is not to be used to instruct. This is a common misunderstanding among new teachers. Instruction and cueing are two separate things. Teachers who use cues to instruct tend to overwhelm and frustrate students. Too much information delivered over the pounding beat of loud music is an ineffective teaching strategy. If your content requires demonstration, this should be done prior to the exercise and not during. If your movement is complex and requires precise form (that your students may be unfamiliar with), you may want to turn off the music, deliver the instruction, then when you turn the music back on, you can cue the changes accordingly.

• Cueing in a Quiet Environment (Read: yoga)

Pleasant cueing in quiet and meditative environments require all the strategies above with the exception of volume and timing cues to the eight-count phrases in a song. While many, if not all, yoga classes play music, the intention is to create a relaxed state of mind. There may be vocals in the music, but its lower volume can be talked over without creating anxiety. The key point I wish to make about cueing a yoga class has to do with the pitch and timbre of your voice. Your voice should be complimentary to the feel of the music, not in competition with it.

Understanding the basic principles of cueing will accelerate your mastery of them. Many teachers do not have the benefit of being trained in these principles. Not many certification programs offer this type of training, so if you come across one that does, jump on it! Otherwise, here they are.

My recommendation is that you practice at home. If you have a friend willing to help you, invite him or her into your practice space and blindfold them (yes, you read that right). Cueing to a blindfolded audience will help you hone your verbal cues with immediate feedback. To hone your non-verbal cues (hand gestures), make sure there is a mirror in front of you so you can watch how your audience responds to you. Use this same dynamic to work on the effectiveness of your voice and hand gestures used together. A little practice goes a long way and a lot of practice goes even further. Cueing is an important skill to develop (key word: develop). Teachers who pay little attention to this skill tend not to do very well. Be one of the great ones. Work on your craft!

Twenty-four

"Tell me and I may forget, teach me and I may
remember, involve me and I will learn"
–Ancient Chinese Proverb

The Final Touch: Visual,
Auditory and Kinesthetic

*T*he *Visual, Auditory and Kinesthetic learning modalities*
were originally identified by psychologists in the 1920s to
understand the most common ways people learn. According to this
theory, most of us prefer to learn in one of three ways: Visual,
Auditory or Kinesthetic, although, in practice, we generally use all
three in varying degrees.

- **Visual:** Visually-dominant learners absorb and retain information
  better when it is presented in imagery, pictures and shapes. They
  learn through seeing and will typically position themselves in
  the front of a classroom for better visibility.

- **Auditory:** Auditory-dominant learners prefer listening to what is being presented. They respond best to verbal instruction: listening, rhythms and tonality.
- **Kinesthetic:** A kinesthetic-dominant learner prefers a physical experience. This person responds well to gestures, body movement, positioning and learns through moving, doing, touching and feeling.

Approximately 65 percent of the population are visual dominant learners, around 30 percent of the population is made up of auditory dominant learners, while Kinesthetic dominant learners are a complex bunch that make up just 5 percent of the population. However, since it may be virtually impossible to discern which of your students have which dominant learning style, the best strategy is to teach to all three.

I was first exposed to these learning modalities during my study of NLP (Neuro Linguistic Programming (a contemporary communication science) back in the late nineties. According to NLP, all three modalities are in constant use. The visual dominant mind sees an image, has a conversation about it (auditory) and then has a feeling about it (kinesthetic). This theory made a lot of sense to me back then, and still does today. Regardless of our dominant learning style, I do believe all three engage concurrently, regardless of the order in which they appear.

The great thing about teaching movement is that all three modalities are organic in a class environment and can be combined in the presentation of the material. If we instruct while we demonstrate, then apply it to music, we've hit all three. We just need to know to do it. A demonstration alone will get through to the 65 percent who are visual dominant learners. But if we add an explanation (arm goes there, leg is extended, hips should be square etc.) we also appeal to the 30 percent who are auditory learners. We've just successfully reached 95 percent of the class (theoretically). If we then explain how the movement feels and connect it to music, we capture the remaining 5 percent who are kinesthetic dominant learners.

The big takeaway here is the opportunity this knowledge affords us. Simply knowing that these modalities exist puts us ahead of the teaching curve. If we apply them to our teaching methods, we are golden!

Here are some examples of how we might do that with the help of several teaching methods:

Demonstration

Explain how the body should be positioned or move and name the muscles which need to be engaged (auditory) as you are demonstrating proper execution (visual). Describe how the movement should feel (kinesthetic).

Mimicry (Follow Along)

While moving, use hand gestures to indicate direction and verbal cues to call out the moves. An example, pointing to the right, while verbally cueing "step touch!"

Correction (Preferably One on One)

Manually adjust the body into the correct position while asking your student to gaze into the mirror to see how the proper placement should look. Explain the muscular mechanics of the exercise.

Repetition, Drills and Consistency

If done in front of a mirror, you only need to add auditory and kinesthetic modalities. Repeat the parameters for the movement or exercise, explaining which muscles should be engaged and add a respective feeling.

Breaking Boundaries

"Future pacing" is a term used to describe the process of taking the imagination into the future. Use this process to create a picture of the desired outcome, describe how the body will achieve it, and draw awareness to how the body feels while doing it.

Modifications

Modifications are a gradual means to an end. Demonstrate the stages of development leading to the desired outcome, explaining the process the body must go through to achieve the full expression of the exercise.

Imagery

The use of imagery is a strong combination of visual, auditory as well as kinesthetic modalities. The auditory description used to evoke imagery often addresses the source of the imagery which can be (and usually is) a feeling.

Exceptional teaching combines:

- Awareness of the Four Responses of the Unfamiliar Mind
- The Nine Teaching Methods
- Proper Cueing
- Visual, Auditory and Kinesthetic modalities

There is a difference between being a teacher and being an instructor. An instructor leads. A teacher teaches. These tools are for teachers. Your content is irrelevant. If your students walk out of your classes having discovered something about themselves or having learned something new, they have been taught. Life is about growth. Sure, if your students have achieved an elevated heart rate and have burned calories, that's an accomplishment worth celebrating. But without the acquisition of knowledge, the accomplishment may not be enough to keep their interest over the long haul. Students want classes they look forward to, that keep them engaged and contribute to their athletic evolution. Be the kind of teacher that champions growth by providing experiences that support it.

This is the complete picture. 90 percent of execution is the knowledge of what to do. The other 10 percent comes with practice. Use these principles to build successful classes in which your students learn, thrive and return for more!

Twenty-five

"The best thing about being a DJ is making people happy.
There is nothing like seeing people get up and dance
or the expression on their face when they hear a song
they love. I also love to educate people on music
they have never heard."
–Chelsea Leyland

Your Playlist

Music can make or break a class. From your students' perspective, the music you play is just as important as the content of your class. Ask anyone who is forced to spend an hour listening to music he or she doesn't like: it's unpleasant.

In today's competitive market, there are many exercise concepts and classes to choose from. If students don't like the music you play, they will go elsewhere, regardless of how wonderful your teaching skills are or how much they like you! The only way around this is to either play your music at a low volume or not play music at all. Considering the motivating power of music and how an inspiring playlist can enhance your class experience, these options aren't very realistic. So, what can you do?

While trying to attract and please everyone is not possible, introducing new music—even if it's only one song on your playlist rotation every week, helps your content feel fresh. It also sends a message to your regular students that your music rotates out

> **" The more creative you are in your choice of music, the greater the perception of artistry in your class.**

frequently. If a disagreeable song (in your student's opinion) appears on your playlist, your students know it won't be on the playlist forever. People will form opinions about songs they've heard. You can circumvent the possibility of playing music someone doesn't like by playing music they haven't yet formed an opinion about.

There is no getting around the use of repetition in the delivery of your content material. It's how the mind and body learn. In light of so much repetition, adding new music to your playlist is your best defense against your students' boredom. Doing the same exercises every week is enough for anybody to grow tired of a workout. But if you counter with an ever- changing, dynamic playlist, your movement may lose some of its repetitive edge.

Here are a few guidelines you can follow when creating your playlist. These guidelines can help you engineer a musical experience that is appropriate for your content, pleasant to listen to, motivating, and inspiring.

Mining Music

Finding great music requires time and effort. If your goal is to add one to two new songs to each of your class playlists every week, you must set aside time in your weekly schedule to search for music and test out your music's compatibility with your content.

Mining music is a hit-or-miss endeavor. In my experience, it goes hot and cold. I can spend an hour sampling songs and not find anything I can use. Other times, it's a bonanza and I may download five or more songs in ten minutes! On other occasions, upon application, the music I've downloaded sounds great but doesn't quite work in my playlist and I'm back to square one. In every regard, mining great music is a time-consuming process that must be factored into your weekly class preparation schedule. Music is of paramount relevance to your class experience. Your playlist sets the tone of your class. You must dedicate time, thought and care to it and this requires effort.

There are several options available for prospecting music. Some teachers use streaming apps, others browse I-tunes and search by artist or genre. Your internet browser is another great source if you're looking for lesser known, award-winning music or for cover songs performed by well known artists. The deeper you search, the more gems you will find. Often I will pull up an album that contains a Top-40 hit and, avoiding that particular song, I'll search for a similar song deeper into the album. I have found great music using this method.

Adding Top-40 hits to your playlist, unless they are "re-mixed" to sound a bit different, is a risky call. The advantage to playing Top-40 hits is students hear the song outside of the studio and may be reminded of your class. The disadvantage is that Top-40 tunes are often overplayed on the airwaves and people tend to tire of them quickly. If you play the song only a few times, that should be fine and can be very exciting for students. But if the song is regularly on your playlist rotation while it's all over the radio, social media and is also being played by other teachers at your studio, the song may "burn out" quickly—this is not a good thing for you!

The more creative you are in your choice of music, the greater the perception of artistry in your class. Teachers who play all Top-40 can give the impression they may not be imaginative with their content either. Avoid commercial hits when possible. There is a copious amount of really great recorded music that doesn't make it onto the charts. Search for it!

Gyms and studios are required to pay royalty fees for the music they and/or their teachers play. Licensing companies like BMI, ASCAP and SESAC require this. I mention this so you can feel confident in playing whatever music you've downloaded from publicly accessible platforms.

Become your own personal DJ. Seek out great music that provides the perfect inspiration or backdrop to your class content. Your playlist should be the icing on the cake!

Criteria for Selecting Music

> { **There are three main criteria for your music selection: a song's tempo, its length and the mood it creates.** }

When selecting music to match the tempo of your exercises, consider the speed of the repetitive movement you have choreographed. Each muscle contraction and release represents a beat. For example, for abdominal crunches, 125–135 beats per minute (BPM) is ideal. However, if you can't move at this tempo, such as executing push-ups for example, you can use the same BPM, but time the contractions in two counts down and two counts up. If this sounds complicated, you can use the tried and true strategy of doing your exercises to the music to determine if there's a good match with the tempo of your song.

Next, take into consideration how long you will be doing a particular exercise. In my Dancer's Stretch class, there's a three to four-minute segment for abdominal work. When I'm ready to change up the song for this segment, I shop for three to four-minute songs that are 125–135 beats per minute.

During the warm-up period in my jazz classes, I always include isolation exercises. It takes me about five minutes to do all of the exercises, so I look for songs that are about five minutes long with 120 beats per minute—which is the perfect tempo for isolation work.

Everybody loves reaping the benefits of sit-ups, push-ups and other strength training exercises, but few enjoy the process. The music you play during these exercises can help make the process more enjoyable. The strong pounding bass line found in electronic dance music (EDM) is ideal to help keep students moving in equal measure repetition. However, during a static passive stretch, a relaxing melody at 72 beats per minute would contribute beautifully to the experience.

A word here about lyrics: They can get you in trouble! Be sure to listen carefully to each song you select! Profanity, a dark message or story, depressing lyrics . . . keep in mind your students **" Your playlist is an expression of your personality and interests.** will be listening! A few years ago, during one of my music searches, I came upon a spellbinding song by one of my favorite artists. The tempo, length and musical composition of the song were perfect for one of my stretches. The vocals were very soulful and full of emotion. When I found this particular song I felt I had hit gold. I was so excited about the instrumentation and composition I didn't fully listen to the lyrics until I played it in class. Avoid doing this! There was nothing I could do without disrupting the class. I had all my students in a relaxing stretch with their eyes closed, listening to a deeply sad and disturbing description of the horrors of drug addiction. Save yourself an experience like this. Listen to your lyrics!

Musical Genres to Generally Avoid

A little common sense and sensibility go a long way regarding which types of musical genres to avoid. There are hundreds of genres and the vast majority are fair game—as long as they are in their proper context. Christian music is beautiful but may not be relatable unless you're teaching in a church where everyone present is of the same faith. Heavy metal is popular among only a certain demographic. If that's your class demographic, go for it. Same goes for Gansta Rap, some Country Music and Gospel . . . Grunge, Gothic Rock, Punk, Holiday music and Folk music. Certainly, adding diverse genres into your playlist can be a very exciting and creative touch. I encourage you to do this. Only be careful about your selections. If you are unsure about how a song may be received, play it for a friend. Or if you notice a negative reaction from your students, remove the song from your playlist.

At the end of the day, your playlist is an expression of your personality and interests. The music you play in class will attract like-minded individuals who share an appreciation for your musical tastes. Not every music genre will appeal to everyone. This is something you must accept and not take personally. Music is a very powerful and personal experience. Some songs conjure up wonderful memories while others can remind us of a painful experience. You have no control over what memories are triggered among your students. Do not take on this responsibility! Choose your music according to the experience you wish to create and be open to feedback. Celebrate your successes, remove the failures and learn from them. Be creative but not over the top!

Twenty-six

"Music is therapy. Music moves people.
It connects people in ways that no other medium can.
It pulls heart strings. It acts as medicine."
–Macklemore

Deconstructing Your Music
To Attach Movement

*P*airing your movement with the musical flow of a song requires you to deconstruct its composition into verses, chorus and bridge while also identifying the song's time signature and phrases. This requires a little bit of knowledge, pen and paper.

Music is composed on a time signature that measures beats per bar or measure. About 95 percent of the songs you are likely to play in your class will have been composed on a four-count bar, also known as a 4/4 measure. Musicians will count these bars as 1-2-3-4, 1-2-3-4, etc. Each number represents a beat. Dancers and choreographers count 4/4 measures in eights. 1-2-3-4-5-6-7-8, grouping two 4-count bars together. A musical phrase contains eight bars (thirty-two counts or beats). In dance, a choreographic phrase contains the same thirty-two counts but they are divided into four, 8-counts. It's the same thing—only viewed differently. A common theory for this is that choreographers use eight counts to facilitate learning longer phrases of movement, while for musicians it's easier to quickly read a four-count measure on a sheet of music. You might notice that musicians count off 1-2-3-4, while dancers count off 5-6-7-8. Both methods cue-up the beginning count of 1 in a bar.

Once you are able to identify the musical phrases in a song, you can anticipate changes in the composition before they happen. Again, most of the music you are likely to play will use the 4/4 time signature. At the end of a thirty-two-count phrase, new instrumentation or percussion typically appears. Depending on the precision of your movement, especially if you are creating dance choreography, being able to pick up on these types of subtle (and sometimes not so subtle) changes in your music can add tremendous depth to the intelligence of your movement.

A count is a beat. To locate the top of a four-count or eight-count measure, you begin counting on the first down beat. In an eight count, the down beat will drop on the first and fifth count. Until you develop precision in identifying the first down beat, listen for the first word in a lyrical sentence. This is not always accurate—as vocals can kick in on virtually any count. But until you develop a sense for hearing the first down beat, you can try this method. Music is very methodical and structured. At some point it will become very easy for you to spot the down beat. It really just takes a little practice.

If your workout moves to a beat it is important that you eventually develop an understanding of time signature, beats, bars and phrases. This will enhance your class experience as your students will feel like they are "dancing" through the exercises. Leading and cueing changes to occur on the down beat is arguably dance—if we define dance as synchronized movement that matches the speed and rhythm of a piece of music.

{ **It doesn't matter if your movement is push-ups, sit-ups or other repetitive exercises. If you are executing them on the count and cohesively with the musical phrasing in a song, you are dancing!** }

The creation of choreography requires a deeper dive into the music you have chosen, specifically if the song you are using has lyrics. Some forms of dance choreography such as lyrical, contemporary and hip hop may follow the story line in a song, requiring you to learn the song lyrics to set movement on the words. Alternatively, as is typically seen in dance fitness choreography, the movement you create must be layered upon the musical phrases, and also be connected to the verses, chorus and bridge in a song. This may strike you as being more complicated, but in actuality, it's easier than it sounds!

Let's take a look at the verses, chorus and bridge of a song. As a general rule, the type of music you are likely to use in your class can be broken down into these three sections. Some songs have intros, pre-choruses, and outros as well, but for the most part, if you just focus on the verse–chorus–bridge structure, you will gain a better understanding of how to pair your movement to each part of a song.

The verses move the story along. The chorus is usually the catchiest part of the song because of its repetition (and usually contains the song title). The bridge is a departure from the verse and chorus, linking the two. The most common song structure is verse–chorus–verse–chorus–bridge–chorus. Once you identify how your song is structured, you should map each section in eight-count phrases. This lets you know how many counts of choreography you have time to do within each section before it changes. Most commonly, the count structure of each of these sections is the same. The lyrics will change from one verse to another; however, the chorus usually contains the same lyrics or similar ones.

{ **When choreographing movement to a particular song, I begin by mapping out the song structure by printing out the lyrics and identifying the different sections.** }

I label each verse, pre-chorus, chorus and bridge with a letter (V,PC,C and B respectively). Next I listen to the song repeatedly, counting the beats in groups of eight. If the song has more than one bridge, I'll label each one separately. The purpose of labeling is to identify the repetitive parts of the song. This gives me the framework for my movement. Dance fitness for example is very repetitive. Each dance move is done to the left then to the right or to the front then to the back: typically, two 8-counts in each direction. If the verse is one musical phrase (thirty-two counts or four 8-counts) I know I must create two 8-counts of movement (done on each side). I will repeat this movement every time a verse is repeated in the song. The same is done with the pre-chorus, chorus and the bridge(s).

This entire process requires less time as you become proficient with it. But in the beginning, it may take you an hour or more to map and choreograph a three-minute song. It really is like anything: Practice makes perfect. As you get into the habit of preparing your classes, you will organically set aside time every week to search for music and to choreograph your movements.

Twenty-seven

"Leadership is not a position or a title,
it is action and example."
–Cory Booker

When Things Go Wrong

W hen do things go wrong? The short answer is: When you least expect it!

You drive across town only to discover you've forgotten your music. The power cuts off in the middle of your class and the room goes dark. A student drops a weight on his/her foot, dislocates a shoulder, pulls a hamstring or sprains an ankle in your class. You trip on your shoelace and face plant while demonstrating a move or you fall out of a turn while explaining how to execute it correctly. A speaker blows. One of your students is rude to another. Someone walks out of your class upset. A student's phone rings, they answer it, and go on talking on the phone while the class is going on. A student brings his or her young children into your class and the kids are running about, disrupting the class, and breaking your concentration. There's an accident on the highway or you get a flat tire and arrive late to class—or not at all. All these things, and worse, have happened to me. If you're ever at a loss for conversation among your peer teachers, ask them to share stories about unexpected things that have happened in their classes. Fun Topic!

Accept the fact that on occasion things will go wrong. The question is not how to avoid the unexpected. The question is: "How will you respond to it?" For all the wisdom I may have gained from these and other experiences, the only answer I have for you is to remain calm. Stay calm and carry on, as they say: The show must go on (if possible)!

If you've forgotten your music, you teach without it or borrow someone else's and improvise. If the power cuts off and no one leaves, your students expect to continue without it and so must you. Address bad behavior with patience, understanding and compassion, but shut it down! When I have fallen in class, I made a joke about it. I tell my class the pressure is off! If the teacher falls and gets up, students have permission to do the same!

Remain calm. Students are aware of what's happening around them. How you handle it affects how they experience it. If you are calm and accepting, they will be too. If you shut down bad behavior, others will be grateful. If someone gets hurt and you show concern and make sure they receive attention, your students will feel safe. If you make a mistake, your students will feel less intimidated about making one themselves. A true leader is not made in a crisis; rather they are defined by how they manage one. Manage the unexpected with class and authority: remain calm!

Twenty-eight

"There is no exercise better for the heart
than reaching down and lifting people up."
–John Homes

Pulling it All Together

*H*ead spinning? Are you feeling a bit overwhelmed by all this information? If so, take a breath. Let's circle back to the big picture.

Your class is comprised of four essential elements (Chapter 13) that can be grouped into three parts:

1. Content
2. Teacher
3. Delivery of Objectives

Content Comes First

You must be trained in your chosen field. You must have the expertise and physicality to deliver the content and you must constantly be updating your encyclopedia of knowledge to incorporate new things.

Next, There's YOU, the Person, the Individual, the Teacher

You must check your little suitcase at the door and open your heart to judge others only when it is constructive and relevant to your content. You must acknowledge your students for the effort they make to attend class and for their trust in what you are asking their bodies to do. You must make your class fun, inspiring and motivating against a rolling backdrop of wonderful music.

Thirdly, There's Your Delivery

You must prepare your classes ahead of time, with a clear understanding of which teaching methods are best suited to your content. You must establish your objectives and fulfill them. You must take care to present your content slowly and repetitively and watch for class cues as to when you should move on. If you'll be absent, you must get a good sub.

Rockstar teachers with mega successful classes do all of the above. Each of these three parts is fully developed in them— and growing. They work at their craft, they spend time fine tuning their classes and they are observant of their mistakes—viewing them as opportunities for improvement. They take other teachers' classes, attend workshops, earn certifications and read books about personal growth and class content. Being a teacher is not a cookie cutter, factory line existence. The classroom is a dynamic and creative environment that is constantly evolving. Great teachers not only stay ahead of the curve, they are at the forefront leading the charge. They achieve this by continuously working on themselves, their content and their delivery. To be an exceptional teacher, these are the things I recommend you do as well!

{ Evolutionary growth creeps in over time, but awareness happens instantly. }

Now that you are aware of the three-part big picture, all that is needed is to color in the details to develop a visual of what you are striving for. Great teaching is a journey with a far off destination, much like life itself. Remember, you can't get to Los Angeles with a map to Miami. Visualize the class and the kind of teacher you want to be. Close your eyes and envision it. Next, plan your journey to get there! How will you stay on top of your content? What teaching methods will you use or perfect over time? What aspects of your personality can you explore to make your classes great fun in addition to being productive?

If you are already teaching, what are you going to do differently in developing your plan? How will you refine your journey? What are you already doing successfully that you want to keep doing? Take a moment to visualize your class, think about what you've learned in these pages, and make a list. In the left column of the table below, list the things you want to keep doing and in the right column, list what you'd like to newly incorporate (in no particular order).

Keep:		Add:	
1.		1.	
2.		2.	
3.		3.	
4.		4.	
5.		5.	

If you are new to teaching, create your plan by making a list of what you've gleaned from these chapters and write out your intentions.

Here's your list:

In regard to myself, I intend to:

1.	
2.	
3.	

The teaching methods I will use are:

1.	
2.	
3.	
4.	

This is your foundation. Start here! Expressing your intentions can help organize your thoughts into a cohesive picture. It can help you "de-clutter" your mind of what you've learned that doesn't necessarily apply to your content. Pick and chose what resonates with you so that you can craft a framework you can work within.

You may or may not have realized this when you decided to enter this profession, but great teaching is an art and a skill. It is a hugely satisfying way to make a living; it's a healthy lifestyle for you and will bring you many moments of joy. There are numerous reasons to want to excel at teaching; the main one is the opportunity to contribute to others. A great class can be the best part of someone's day and you are front and center making that happen.

PART 3
The Business Side of Teaching

Twenty-nine

"Luck is what happens when preparation
meets opportunity."
–Seneca

Combining Inner Wisdom and Business Knowledge

Welcome to Part 3: The Business Side of Teaching! Just when you might think we've covered just about everything you need to know to create and deliver an exceptional class experience . . . wait, there's more! The journey continues! Only now, we will look at how the knowledge acquired in Part 1 and 2 (your inner work) fits into an (outer) professional environment. Hello, Part 3!

But first, let's review a few things.

In Part 1 of this book, "The Journey Begins with Us", we took a look inward to recognize our personal approach to the world. We learned that by understanding ourselves, we are able to become aware of the "window" through which we see, perceive and respond to others. Part 1 asked you to embark upon a process of evolvement, growth, and transformation of the self. The journey you went through was necessary in order to discover your own uniqueness and how your perspective informs your statement of purpose.

Part 2, "Your Class", is the unfolding of the process of creating not just any class but a successful, unique and productive experience for your students. The structuring of content and the application of the strategies revealed in this part are put into practice from the perspective of having gone through the process of evolving the self and establishing a statement of purpose after Part 1. In part 2 the practical "secrets" of creating a successful class are revealed. That part contains the more technical aspect of teaching.

> **The knowledge acquired in Part 1 and Part 2 should be your internal anchor. Part 3 prepares you to understand the professional environment.**

Now comes Part 3 connecting the work and the knowledge acquired during the "inner" preparation from Part 1 and 2 and the "outer" business system (the work environment with its regulations, policies, taxes, marketing and advertising strategies, resume, people, social and professional obligations, etc.).

The knowledge acquired in Part 1 and Part 2 should be your internal anchor. By developing a clear vision of the self (Part 1), identifying purpose (Part 1) and strategically structuring and creating a unique class (Part 2), you can live, express and fulfill your purpose. And when you are ready to face the outer environment, the clarity you've acquired will help to keep you centered, focused, and empowered.

Part 3 prepares you to understand the professional

environment. You will be exposed to the different business aspects of cooperating and/or partnering with a professional and successful studio or what could be other work environments. You will learn about the challenges and rewards of a successful studio, how to select your employers or business partners and how you yourself can become a successful business partner or employee.

My purpose in Part 3 is to make you aware of both sides of the business: that of the studio and that of the teacher, so you may navigate these waters gracefully and successfully.

Thirty

"We are not a team because we work together.
We are a team because we trust, respect and
care for each other."
–Vala Asfhar

Harmony:
Understanding the Teacher/Studio
Business Relationship

I think it's safe to say that everyone who enters into a business collaboration does so with good intentions, mainly with the expectation of it leading to a harmonious relationship. Successful collaboration is definitively a joint effort to accomplish a pre-defined goal or goals. In order for the collaboration to be successful it is important that the partners involved show mutual respect, a desire for cooperation, and a willingness to contribute to a win-win-win (studio, teacher, and student) outcome.

I believe that, for the most part. Although good intentions can be a foundation for a healthy work relationship between a teacher and a studio, clarity about the boundaries and responsibilities that define a business relationship can help avoid possible misunderstandings and lead to a harmonious and successful partnership. There is a quirky dynamic prevalent among boutique fitness studios where some teachers are hired as W-2 employees and others are hired as independent contractors (Form 1099). These types of collaboration determine different work relationships. In the next paragraphs I will explain to you the differences between the two. It is my hope your understanding of these employment relationships will help avoid confusion, misunderstanding and the risk of a collaboration ending bitterly. Clarity on this subject may instead lead you to empowerment, improving your decision-making process because you will be familiar with the parameters of your employment status.

> ❝ **A 1099 independently contracted teacher and a W-2 employed teacher play different positions on the team. They are both team players, but their roles are different.**

A 1099 Form and a W-2 Form are separate tax forms for two different types of workers. Collaboration with a 1099 Form establishes that the teacher has entered the business relationship as an independent contractor. Taxes will not be deducted from the paycheck but he/ she must report self-employment income. Collaboration with a W-2 Form means the teacher is an employee of the studio, he/she receives a salary, and taxes will be deducted from the paycheck, according to the W-4 form he/she completed at hiring. A W-4 is a tax form that is used to calculate the amount of federal income tax withheld from paychecks based on the information disclosed when hired which include marital status, allowances and exemptions. Every one of these tax forms not only has different tax ramifications, but also each establishes and dictates a different type of work relationship with the studio.

A 1099 independently contracted teacher and a W-2 employed teacher play different positions on the team. They are both team players, but their roles are different.

> ## A W-2 employed teacher is considered staff or faculty. A studio places certain expectations on these teachers.

They may be trained to work the front desk and engage in other administrative duties. They also typically teach a larger number of weekly classes, participate in staff meetings and are privy to the inner workings of the studio. These individuals may be considered to be "lead" teachers who assist the studio with hiring and training other teachers. They are commonly considered to be exclusive to the studio, restricted from teaching at other competing studios. W-2 employed teachers may be considered studio "ambassadors" who may also participate in the marketing efforts of the studio. Their employment with the studio is governed by labor laws which frequently include limited vacation pay, benefits (health insurance, 401k, etc.), worker's compensation insurance, and unemployment benefits. These teachers may be subject to annual performance reviews and pay raises as would be expected from any W-2 employment. Compensation for W-2 teachers may be calculated based upon classes taught, hours worked, or most commonly, both. W-2 status can be full or part-time. The bottom line here is that a W-2 constitutes a greater teacher commitment to the studio and a vested interest in its overall success (not solely limited to the classes he/she teaches).

A 1099 independently contracted teacher is a "service provider" for the studio. In other words, the studio is a "client" of the teacher, not their employer. This is a huge distinction! These teachers are typically self-employed, often they are responsible for having their own health and liability insurance, establishing their own individual pension and/or unemployment plan. A studio hires independently contracted teachers to provide a service to its members. Parameters are given to communicate expectations (as outlined in the Independent Contractor Agreement which is signed at hiring) and if these expectations are not met, both the studio and the independent contractor may terminate the contract at will.

Additionally, an independent contractor/teacher has no legal recourse for being terminated from a studio: there are no unemployment benefits, unused paid vacation or severance pay upon termination (unless the studio offers it as a gesture of thanks and goodwill).

> The only job "security" for a 1099 teacher is to consistently and professionally meet the predefined expectations expressed at the time of hiring or through periodic reviews and updates.

A studio is not responsible for the success of the classes taught—that responsibility falls on the teacher. This is not to say that a studio will not work in partnership with the teacher to market and promote his/her classes to members. Most often marketing is (and should be) a joint effort; I will go into this topic extensively in Chapter 35: "Marketing and Managing Your Class Successfully: Get the Word Out". However, with a 1099 teacher, the buck stops with them. The studio provides a member base upon which teachers may draw students. The studio may brand, promote and offer special deals for students, but ultimately, if the teacher fails to fulfill the terms of the contract, the studio may elect to cease to be the teacher's client and terminate the contract. Other possible reasons that may lead to the termination of the contract are: Violations such as excessive absences, poor attitude, unprofessional behavior, delivering a substandard class experience, failure to maintain a minimum average of students per class, excessive tardiness, misconduct, student complaints, etc. Most studios will give a warning, verbal, written or both; however, if any of these conditions persist, the teaching contract will likely be terminated. Note: these conditions may also trigger the termination of a W-2 teacher—so in this regard, the ethical and professional code of conduct is the same for both a 1099 and a W-2 teacher.

But, take heart! The advantages of a 1099 contract weigh heavily in favor of the teacher over the studio. An independently contracted teacher has greater freedom to teach at multiple studios, freedom to take vacation days multiple times during the year, freedom to sub out classes whenever necessary and freedom from having to comply with studio requests for additional classes or to participate in studio events. The independent contractor may still be asked for help with marketing the studio as a whole, but he/she has the choice to accept or decline. However, I would advise to be mindful of this level of freedom because it does not exempt a teacher from fulfilling the contract expectations nor from managing absences in a professional manner.

Ultimately, frequent absences, ignoring studio emails, being uninformed about studio activity, failure to respect the confidentiality of studio emails, teaching indiscriminately all over town and failure to support the studio's efforts to promote itself as a whole may reflect poorly on the teacher's class attendance which may then place the relationship with that studio in jeopardy. Working as

> " **A teacher's professionalism, whether as a W-2 or a 1099, does not go unnoticed.**

an independent contractor can be very rewarding as long as the teacher fully understands that the studio is his/her client and as with any other "provider/client" relationship, the client is free to let the service provider go if the services rendered lose their value or if the independent contractor's behavior reflects poorly on the studio. Independent contractors are independent. However, they do not exist in a bubble. They must still be a team player with the understanding that the overall well-being of the studio is beneficial for all and any effort to help the studio remain strong only benefits everyone—themselves included. At the end of the day, professionalism rules the roost—W-2 or 1099. Many studios are small businesses that came into being as a result of someone's dream. Studio owners tend to be lovers of what they do. Studio staff, faculty and independent contractors are often considered "family" and are treated as such. There may even be an intimate, casual and "anti-corporate" like atmosphere, but this doesn't mean the studio doesn't have business responsibilities to watch the bottom line in order to meet rent and payroll on time. A teacher's professionalism, whether as a W-2 or a 1099, does not go unnoticed. Teachers who understand a studio's obligations to its other teachers, staff, as well as to its members, are a joy to work with. Teachers who have this mindset are greatly appreciated. Be one of them!

Thirty-one

"Always define WHAT you want to do with your life
and WHAT you have to offer to the world . . . "
–Richard N. Bolles

Self-Marketing:
Tips for Creating a Professional Bio
and Resume

Your resume and bio are powerful self-marketing mediums intended to advertise and sell your services. They are written for two different audiences. A resume communicates your value and your factual professional achievements either in a chronological or functional format to a potential employer. It is a reflection of your training, your accomplishments, and what you can and wish to contribute to a studio A bio is a promotional summary of you, usually written in third person as an essay or a story, to your students. It communicates not only your values but also your background, the highlights of your accomplishments and achievements. Resumes are written for employers. Bios are written for students, your audience. By understanding this distinction you have already taken the first step in creating a successful resume and bio for your dream teaching job. Each document should be crafted with its reader in mind.

Let's start with what a teaching resume should include:

- Name and contact information.
- Objective or Career Goal. (State your clear intentions)
- Highlights/Summary of Qualifications or Outstanding Achievements (if available).
- State the best of your career, most impressive moments and/or achievements
- (Professional) Experience. (Who you worked for and classes taught.)
- Education or Training. (Write a summary of your education and training experience.)

❝ Resumes are written for employers. Bios are written for students, your audience.

A teaching resume should not only contain information about your training, education, special skills and work history; it should also include a list of all the classes you are qualified to teach. Provide a description of each class concept including its objectives. Do not assume a potential employer can figure out where your expertise lies based upon your training and certifications. By removing the guess work and listing all your unique class concepts you will set yourself apart from other applicants. The greater the variety of classes you can teach, the greater the opportunity to be hired full-time or be given multiple weekly classes at any given studio. At dance 101, if a teacher specifies that he/she can teach tap, ballet, jazz, modern, barre and stretch, I will take a very close look at him/her. This teacher could potentially be a tremendous asset—

not only in terms of how many classes they could teach, but they might also be a great sub. Don't be modest with your resume; let it reflect your uniqueness and professionalism. Flaunt your variety! It's valuable!

A great strategy for composing your resume is to put yourself into a studio owner's shoes. If you were the one hiring, what would you want to know about "you", the candidate? Most likely you would want to know: Does he/she have the training? How much experience does he/she have? How successful are his/her classes (or have been)? Is he/she actively involved with the marketing of classes, and if yes, how? Does he/she understand the business aspect of teaching? What value would he/she bring to the studio? These are definitively the things I am interested in learning about a candidate. Most teaching resumes I've seen do not address these questions, opting to simply list employment. While this is important information to know, does it send me running to the phone to call this person? Would it you? This chapter is not about crafting a resume like everyone else's. If you are interested in crafting a resume that will set your uniqueness apart, read on.

When listing your classes, include a brief description of each and its objectives (you may refer back to Part 2, Chapter 14: "Setting Objectives Matters", for more details), also indicate their frequency (once a week, twice a week, etc.), add the average attendance (e.g., ten to fifteen people), and finally indicate the size of the classroom. Listing this information shows you are sensitive to the business side of teaching. How often a class repeats

> **" A great strategy for composing your resume is to put yourself into a studio owner's shoes. If you were the one hiring, what would you want to know about "you", the candidate?**

each week can indicate its level of success without you having to boast about it. If a class meets twice a week, that already says something. Studios often track attendance as an indication of the health of the class. Adding class frequency and attendance averages to your resume will further set you apart from any other candidate. This is a practice I've rarely seen (ok, never); however, from a studio owner perspective, this would take away much of the guess work, and position you as a very strong candidate!

A word to the wise: do not embellish. This can get you in a lot of trouble and may result in a short-lived position if you even make it past the audition. I have auditioned teachers with very impressive resumes that included a long list of recent performances with notable choreographers and out-of-state dance companies. But the thing about the physical arts is whereas it may be easy to embellish on paper, how a teacher moves clearly demonstrates their level of training. There's no fudging that. Technique or lack thereof, is apparent to the eye. In these cases, I would wonder how on earth these people could have had these opportunities when they clearly didn't have the training to do so. Needless to say, I thanked these candidates for the audition but did not offer them a position.

> **When you embellish you set the bar higher than you may be able to deliver. There is no fooling someone who has more experience than you.**

In many instances, studios hire for potential. Being new to teaching is not a negative for many studios! If you are new to teaching and the bulk of your experience has been subbing other people's classes, say so. List these classes on your resume. This will tie in with your opening statement about being ready to teach your own classes and looking for the opportunity to do so.

The purpose of your resume is to communicate what you are capable of delivering. This in turn establishes your studio's expectations of you. When the relationship between these two is in balance, it sets the tone for a harmonious teacher/studio relationship going forward.

Your bio is a personal statement about who you are. It may contain historical information about where you are from, as well as your training and accomplishments. But it should also include a narrative about how you feel about your classes, what you love about them, why you love to teach, and what is unique about you or your journey as a teacher. Your bio should communicate your identity as a teacher. It may contain information about your teaching style that is unique to you (music, attitude, feeling, etc.). Personalize your bio by including information that may not be related to your classes, but helps to define you as a person. You can include hobbies, pets, special interests, causes you support or a surprising and interesting fact about you. Keep in mind your bio will likely be published on the studio website (along with your photograph), and possibly on the studio's social media. It may also be used to market your class.

If you are not comfortable writing your bio, ask a friend to help you. The studio should not write your bio—they won't do you justice! Enlist the help of someone who knows you! The best bios I've ever read make me want to know that person! Teachers are an interesting bunch. They tend to be creative souls who live holistic, healthy lifestyles. They are typically seekers who have amassed interesting experiences that are worth sharing. I can't think of a single exception to this. You may not think of yourself in these terms—but your friends do.

> **Personalize your bio by including information that may not be related to your classes, but helps to define you as a person.**

Ask them to help you craft a bio that reflects your soul. Or write it yourself. Either way, be transparent and genuine as to who you are. That's what makes a fantastic bio that is a joy to read.

Thirty-two

"Courage is grace under pressure"
–Ernest Hemingway

Landing the Job

*L*anding a teaching position at a high profile, well managed and popular studio not only increases your chances of a positive and enjoyable work environment, it also reflects powerfully on your teaching resume. Teachers thrive in well-managed studios whose core values embrace excellence and professionalism. This is why it looks so good on your resume! Securing a teaching position at a studio of this caliber does not happen by accident, nor by minimum effort. Care must be taken to identify these studio gems and court them appropriately. They will be selective! Asking "Are you hiring?" will not get you in the door. Nor will years of experience and impressive training guarantee you the job. You must show initiative, interest and present yourself in integrity with who you are as a person and what you bring to the table.

{ **This chapter is not just about finding employment; it is about finding your dream teaching job.** }

Also it contains a step by step approach to doing so. But first, let me begin with a story . . . .

When my daughter turned 17, we both agreed it was time for her to get a part-time job. I jumped at the opportunity to teach her another life lesson, rolled up my sleeves and devised a plan. I knew she didn't have any clue about finding a job, where to start or how to go about it, so I approached the lesson by deconstructing the process into three parts:

1. Prospecting where to work.
2. Asking for an interview.
3. Nailing the interview and getting hired.

But before we could get to any of that, she needed a resume. Given her lack of work history, I knew she would have to be trained at whatever job she got, so we crafted her resume around her willingness to learn and included her grade point average. We put together her character references, listed her extracurricular activities, hobbies, interests and anything else we could think of that would portray her friendly and outgoing nature.

Next, we worked on the interview process. I believed her strongest suits (from an employer's perspective) would be her dependability and her willingness to take direction so I made sure she remembered to mention these things in the interview. I queried her like she was applying for a job, asking the types of questions I anticipated she might get. We role-played during our mock interviews and when I felt she was ready, we moved on to the next lesson: how to prospect a job and how to approach a potential employer.

Since she was interested in applying for a retail position, I suggested she enter a prospective store as a customer. She was to browse and observe how the employees interacted with her and each other. If the employees were happy, attentive and friendly, that might be an indication of good management. I wanted her to tap into how the store made her feel. Did she like the merchandise, the displays and the music they played? This would be the environment she would spend long hours in—did she feel comfortable in it? If so, she was to approach an employee to ask if he/she enjoyed working there and if that went well, she was to ask to speak to the manager if available. If the manager was not available, she would ask if she could return at a later time. She was not to ask if they were hiring! Nor was she to leave her resume. Once face to face with the

" Life is too short to unknowingly place yourself in the wrong environment.

manager, I suggested she break the ice with sincere compliments about the store. She was to be absolutely genuine and specific about what she had observed during her browsing. From there the conversation would continue and she would reveal her interest in a job there. She was to convey that she had reliable transportation, the hours she was available to work and why she wanted to work there (among the other points she was prepared to make).

The day finally arrived and I drove her to the mall. She didn't say much during the drive —but that might have been because I was talking a mile a minute and she couldn't get a word in. I was so proud of her and I wanted her to know how special she was. I drove up to the mall entrance, gave her a kiss, and asked her not to call me until she had a job. Side note here: this may sound harsh, but I knew she'd do well and I wanted her to learn that no matter what life throws at her, she would always know how to get a job (I also didn't want her to quit upon her first rejection).

About three hours later, my phone rang. A very excited voice screamed into the line: "Mom come get me!! I have a job!!" Mission accomplished, lesson learned. My daughter would never go hungry. I exhaled!

One of the great things about being a parent is the opportunity to learn from our children. Up until this point when my daughter was ready to find employment, I had not given this much thought to the process of finding a job. Honestly, I wish I had been able to take my own advice when I was younger and in her position. My early approach to finding a job was the proverbial: "Are you hiring?" question, which is such a put-off to me today. I didn't think much about the job I was asking for; I just wanted to be employed! It wasn't until I became an employer that I realized:

- Companies are most always hiring when it comes to the right person and . . .
- I could be and should be selective and proactive about where I work and for whom.

The lesson I put together for my daughter became a lesson for me too. At some point in your teaching career (hopefully sooner than later) you will have achieved a level of proficiency that allows you to pick and choose where you want to teach. You may even find yourself being courted by a studio. Sitting in the driver's seat of your career (while a great accomplishment), is not a destination; you still have to land the job.

Take an analytical look at the studio or gym you are considering. Ask yourself: Is it a good fit for you? Would you feel comfortable there? Is this a studio or gym you believe in and feel excited and passionate about? Try to get a picture of the studio culture and what might be of value to the prospective studio owner. What is their perspective and what would they hire for? How would you best present yourself and the class(es) you wish to teach? How should you approach and ask for an interview? Furthermore, and most importantly, please keep in mind that the greater the effort you put into getting the job the greater the likelihood you will succeed.

Research the company before you knock on their door. Study their website, research their online presence. Look at their videos and photographs. Follow them on social media. Talk to teachers and/or people who work there. Experience the studio as a student. Take one or more or many of their classes. When you get the interview, you'll be able to speak knowledgeably about the studio and this carries a lot of weight. If I had to choose between two candidates of equal training and one of them could talk knowledgeably about my company—that would be the one I'd pick.

The more you know about a studio, the more on point your interview questions will be. When I interview a potential teacher and he/she has nothing to ask me, I wonder why? How could it be possible not to have any questions? Employment is a commitment. I

> **Take an analytical look at the studio or gym you are considering. Ask yourself: Is it a good fit for you?**

have plenty of questions before I agree to invite someone onto my team, and a strong candidate will have plenty of questions for me too. I understand some people are shy around someone they don't know. But in the context of a teaching position, I am not looking for a shy person! If they are shy with me, how can I expect them to be any different in their classes? Be inquisitive. Prepare a list of questions based upon your research and ask the questions!

Many of our best teachers came to us initially as students. In fact, we often recruit teachers from our student population because they have a deeper understanding of the studio culture. This is a valuable asset that can translate

> **" The more you know about a studio, the more on point your interview questions will be.**

into successful classes because they know their audience! Teachers and studios who "are their customers" first, bring greater wisdom and empathy for the community they serve—a huge hiring plus!

Do your homework and in the process it will become crystal clear if any particular studio is where you should be. Life is too short to unknowingly place yourself in the wrong environment. Chances are if you enjoy the studio as a student, you will enjoy teaching there. Management trickles down from owner(s) to staff to teachers to students. It is highly unlikely you will find happy students but unhappy teachers, or unhappy students but happy teachers. Energy and attitude are contagious. That said, we are all human and have bad days or go through bad periods. If you're researching a studio, rely on your overall experience—not on any one given teacher or student—but on the whole.

Understanding the Perspective of the Studio

A studio owner must have (and will hire) two types of staff: administrative and income- producing. Administrative positions are: front desk, management, back office, social media marketing and customer service, etc. Income-producing positions are teachers and sales people. Depending on the size of the studio, there may be some overlapping of these positions. A manager in a small studio may also handle sales, customer service and social media marketing in addition to managing subs, cancellations, hiring, etc. Teachers may be asked to sign in their classes (front desk). Larger studios typically have greater resources and too much activity going on to overlap positions. They tend to hire with laser proficiency in specific areas. However, when approaching a smaller studio, the more you bring to the table the greater your value to the studio. If you are also trained in studio scheduling software, are good at social media and have customer service skills, make sure you say so!

The studio owner's perspective is one of efficiency. They may fall in love with your personality and enthusiasm, but ultimately they will look at you through a lens of dollars and cents. They have to! If this sounds cold and impersonal, you may not realize the pressure studio owners are under to cover the operating expenses of their studio. Rent alone can eat up to 40 percent of a studio's expenses. Then there's payroll, insurance, maintenance, repairs, utilities, phones, internet service, website, advertising, marketing, supplies, music royalties, accounting services, cost of merchandise, etc. There's a long list of expenses and a lot is at stake. When a studio goes out of business, that owner may also lose his/her house. It's important you understand this.

> **When a studio owner looks at a potential teacher, what goes through the owner's mind is whether or not that teacher will produce and deliver a class that students will pay to take.**

The more you do to convince the studio that you can build a class and deliver an excellent experience, the more appealing you will be. Studios look for staff members that are more like partners than subordinates. They'll ask themselves: "Do I want/need this person on my team? Will he/she be a resource or a drain?" Empathy for your studio's perspective will only strengthen your candidacy and if hired, solidify your position on the team.

How Best to Approach a Studio Owner

Ask for the opportunity. Once you know who the owner or manager is, make your intention and interest known to them. Studio owner/ managers are busy people. If you call and leave a message, you may not get a call back anytime soon. Calling again can be awkward. Your best strategy is to visit the studio in person. However, surprise visits are seldom welcomed and are often intrusive. You should be considerate of this in your initial approach. Do not expect an instant interview, but be prepared just in case. Present yourself with the simple intention to make a human connection. "I just wanted to shake your hand and introduce myself so you'll be able to put a face with the resume, bio and teaching reel that I'm about to send you." Do not linger unless invited.

{ **Studio owners and managers may be crazy busy people, but believe me; they don't want to miss an opportunity to hire a great teacher.** }

In the ten seconds you introduced yourself you already made a good impression. You showed interest by taking the time to come by, you demonstrated great consideration for management by respecting their time, and you came across as being confident.

The Question You Should Never Ask

Personally, I have a 100 percent batting record for turning away any stranger who asks me if I am hiring (even though that was my modus operandi when I was younger). "Are you hiring?" triggers an automatic "no, I'm sorry" from me. I believe this is the most unproductive question anyone can ask a prospective employer, in my opinion. It reveals nothing about the individual or whether he/

she has anything of value to contribute to the company. Further, it indicates a low standard—as in, this individual is just looking to work for anyone who is hiring. It can also demonstrate a lack of interest in the company itself. Studio owners want to hire people who believe in their company's mission and care about the work they do (not just getting paid for it). "Are you hiring?" is a closed ended question. If the response is no, the conversation ends and any attempt to restart it can be awkward. Try not to ask any closed ended questions when you approach a potential employer!

What to Send and How

Once you've personally introduced yourself, email your information. Do not drop off a hard copy with hopes it reaches the right person. Paper gets tossed or it may not reach its destination. Email is permanent (even if it's deleted, it can be retrieved) and you can request a return receipt. Furthermore, email allows you to embed links to your work. If you do not have a video sample of your class, please make one. (You can use your phone camera, but take care to make it presentable. A professional grade production would be wonderful, but may be overkill. A studio will be looking at content, not production quality—unless of course, it's careless and sloppy.) Attach your bio, resume, any certifications or diplomas you may have and include your photograph (the photograph will help associate you with your visit). In the body of your email, you can write something personal about yourself, why you love to teach, what is special about your class and why you want to teach at that particular studio. Be succinct. Try to limit your comments to a few paragraphs on a single page. Close your email with a request for an interview/audition.

A word about your cover email: this is your introduction and the first thing that will be read. Although you may already have introduced yourself in person, your cover email is part two of the first impression you are making. Take a moment to write a customized message. I can't stress this enough. "Canned" cover letters are impersonal and easy to spot. Again, from the studio perspective they are looking for someone who wants to work there, not someone who just wants a job anywhere. Here is an example of a cover letter that would blow my mind (I'd likely decide to hire this person even before meeting him/her or looking at the attachments!).

Dear Ofelia,

It was such a pleasure to meet you the other day. I felt fortunate to have caught you as I know you are very busy running such a successful and beautiful studio!

As promised, attached is my information. I attended a few of your classes last week and felt myself swept up in the positive energy of your space! I can see that you take great care in hiring your teachers as each one I experienced gave an excellent class. I also chatted with a few of your students and I enjoyed hearing how much they love the studio. I was so impressed!

Your studio feels like home to me. I would love to teach for you and I believe my class would contribute a kindred loving energy compatible with the other classes on your schedule. I love to teach; it fills my heart. Giving myself, my knowledge and training to others enriches my life. I would love the opportunity to do this for your students and I would love to be on your team of exceptional teachers.

I look forward to seeing you again. Please let me know when would be your earliest opportunity for an interview/ audition. I presently have good availability—but that can change quickly (as you know!).

With warmest regards,
Your Name here, Future dance 101 Teacher!! :)

I'm not sure if you need me to explain why this letter would impress the heck out of me and what it tells me about the person who wrote it. But, in the event you don't see what I see in these words, this is what this letter communicates to me:

This person:
1. Is respectful of my hard work and considerate of my time—and would be a pleasure to work with because of it.
2. Magnanimously understands that he/she would be part of a team—not a diva in the spotlight.
3. Is selective about where he/she works—as evidenced by taking the time to visit the studio and take classes. Work environment matters to this person, who therefore may likely strive to create a pleasant environment for his/her students.
4. Loves to teach, therefore his/her heart is invested—indicating they would teach passionately and that is a great indication that his/her class would be appreciated and enjoyed by students.
5. Is very professional in his/her communication and would be a good reflection on my studio.
6. Is confident in his/her ability to bring value to the studio.

Lastly, there is nothing more impressive to a potential new employer than a letter of recommendation from a previous one. Easier said than done; I get it. This requires you to keep a level head at the end of a studio relationship (which can be a very emotional time) in order to ask for a letter. Exiting a studio gracefully is covered in Chapter 38, but for the purposes of helping you land a great teaching position, I'd be remiss not to mention it here. When possible, do what you can to exit with a letter. The benefit to having one may greatly outweigh the asking.

Here's your checklist for a successful presentation:
1. Email cover letter (one page)
2. Links to video(s)
3. Bio (your history)
4. Resume (work history, one to two pages)
5. Photograph
6. Letters of recommendation
7. Certifications, diplomas, certificates of completion

In closing, be sure your email has an electronic signature that contains any designations you have, contact phone number, website and/or social media addresses. If you do not have a professional email, create one. Do not use an unprofessional sounding email address!

Going to all this trouble sends a loud message to the studio owner that you are willing to "work the job" even before you are hired! If you are willing to put this much effort just for the opportunity to ask for work, you give the impression that you will work just as hard and diligently when you are actually hired. I know I've quoted this before, but it is useful to always remember:

 How you do anything is how you do everything. –T. Harv Eker

Preparing for the Interview/Audition

Congratulations! You've landed an interview/audition. Now you should prepare for it. Hopefully you've already taken a discerning look at your social media presence before you sent over your resume. It is widely believed that 56–70 percent of employers will look at the social media presence of potential employees before hiring them. Scroll through your posts for anything that might not portray you favorably in the eyes of a studio. Assume the studio is going to take a look. If you consider that the purpose of the interview process is for the studio to get to know you and you them, your online identity can be very revealing. From your research into the studio's social media you learned about their voice in the community. The same holds true for you.

Use your social media to post videos of your classes, foster community among your students and provide examples of your work to the world. Before you post anything, ask yourself: Is it true? Is it kind? Is it necessary? Is it a good reflection on you? I hesitate to even mention this (because it is common sense) but the things I've seen some teachers post have astonished me.

It is likely you may be asked about the work you did at your previous studio. Always portray your experience at another studio in a positive light. Even if you are angry, no matter the circumstances, never speak ill of your former studio or studio manager/owner. Doing so may cost you the job you are interviewing for. You may think your potential employer would surely agree with your side

> **If you are willing to put this much effort just for the opportunity to ask for work, you give the impression that you will work just as hard and diligently when you are actually hired.**

of the story (if they knew all the "facts") but in his/her mind he/she may be thinking this is how you will someday talk about him/her (even if they do agree with you!). Plus, if you're carrying anger towards your former employer, your potential new employer might be concerned that you'd bring that negative energy into his/her studio (another reason not to hire you). In summary, try not to let a bad experience sabotage your future and all you've worked to create for yourself. Vent all you want to your closest friends—just not on your social media and not to any potential new employer.

If possible, dress for the interview as you would to teach

your class. As the saying goes: "Dress for the job you want." This gives the studio an opportunity to visualize you in that position.

Prepare a list of questions. This demonstrates that you are thoughtful and careful with your commitments. When a studio offers you a position, it needs to know it can count on you to meet expectations. Save your questions for the end as some of them may have already been answered during the interview. Here are some examples of questions you may want to ask, if they haven't already been addressed:

1. What is the studio policy regarding subs and cancellations?
2. What time am I expected to arrive at the studio?
3. Do you have a non-compete radius? If so, what is it?
4. Am I permitted and encouraged to market my class on my personal social media?
5. Do you encourage teachers to friend or connect with students on social media?
6. How will you announce/launch my class?
7. Will you continue to market my class on an on-going basis? If so, how can I help?
8. Am I permitted to comp potential new students into my class?
9. Does the studio have any restrictions or preferences regarding the music I play in class?
10. In addition to teaching my class, are there other expectations of me?
11. Is there a minimum or maximum number of classes I would be required to teach?
12. How many students do I need to average for my class to be considered successful? Is there a minimum number required to teach a class?
13. Will I be issued a W-2 or a 1099?

Notice I did not include a question about compensation.

Compensation is best discussed after the offer has been made. How much compensation is offered to you may be influenced by the perceived value you bring to the studio based upon your training, **«« Always portray your experience at another studio in a positive light.** experience, interview, and audition. If you ask too soon, you may deny the studio the opportunity to think through their best offer (more on this in Chapter 33).

The audition process varies from studio to studio and genre to genre. A rule of thumb is to always ask (never assume) what is expected from you in an audition. Some studios will simply ask you to teach a class to another teacher, an owner, a manager or a small group of teachers. Depending on your experience, some studios may ask you to sub a class and observe you. This process varies so greatly, the best course of action is to ask how to prepare (if studio management has not already prepped you). Be very specific in your questions: how much time will you have? What specifically do they want to see (i.e. everything you are capable of teaching or something specific)? Whatever instructions are given you, follow them to the letter! Be sure to arrive ten minutes early and ready to go!

Lastly, be sure to bring hard copies of what you emailed. This may not be necessary, but is an appreciated touch.

Bottom line, interviewing for a job can be a challenge on both sides. Like speed dating, each party has a limited amount of time to gather information about each other! Everybody is nervous because a big decision lies in the balance and a poor choice (on either side) may have unpleasant consequences. Invariably, there's a lot of second guessing after the fact. Both candidate and employer may replay the interview for the "woulda, shoulda, coulda" asked this or said that. Or worse, one may regret offering the job or accepting the position.

My best advice for you is to do your homework, put together a package of information that does you justice and relax as much as you can during the interview/audition. Be prepared and you will do well. Be yourself and you'll be hired for who you truly are. And remember: just as you are being interviewed so too are you doing the interviewing.

Thirty-three

"Seek first to understand, then to be understood."
–Dr. Stephen R. Covey

How to Negotiate Compensation

Fourteen years of hiring teachers under my belt, I have some stories! (That's another book.) Some consider the ability to negotiate an art. To be honest, it only requires an understanding of the perspective of who is sitting across the table from you.

"Big Box" gyms and large corporately owned boutique studios (chain or franchise) may have a strict compensation schedule that has little room for negotiation on the front end. At these establishments, raises may be given over time and influenced by periodic performance reviews. However, smaller owner operated studios may have greater flexibility when it comes to teacher compensation. Regardless of who is offering you a position, the "secret" to negotiating compensation is to have an understanding of a studio's business model. Studio income is driven by attendance. The greater the number of students you attract and retain in your classes, the more money you generate for the studio. The more you generate, theoretically the more you should be paid. A teacher's financial worth is driven by numbers. A well trained and qualified teacher who averages five to ten students per class will be compensated according to the average revenue this class generates for the studio. Compensation is driven by economics, not by resume. However, the greater the training and experience, the greater likelihood the class will attract a larger number of students. If you would like to earn a specific amount of compensation for your class, you must look at the business side of your craft.

> " The "secret" to negotiating compensation is to have an understanding of a studio's business model.

The economy of a studio, like any other business, is determined by ratios. For every dollar collected, a certain percentage goes to rent, another to teacher pay, another to administrative salaries, another to expenses, and another to net income (profitability). If your class generates an average attendance revenue of $200, your compensation may be calculated as a percentage of this amount. There are two factors that drive that $200: attendance and pricing. If you take a position with a studio that charges its members a low rate per class, the revenue per class will be lower and this in turn will impact your compensation.

{ **The survival of a studio is directly tied to its "income to expense" ratios.** }

It really is that simple. Teachers who understand this will know how to successfully negotiate compensation. Those who mistakenly focus on the appearance of a studio and the success of other classes as a barometer for how much compensation they should request will likely be disappointed. This approach is greatly flawed. A well managed studio must look at each class independently. If anything, look at the appearance of a studio and the success of other classes as an indication of your potential earnings as obviously such a lovely and popular studio will have a large student base from which you may draw and build your classes!

Armed with this knowledge, the business aspect of your new class should be a topic of conversation once you've been offered a position (not before). Studios typically offer a lower starting pay to begin with until they get their bearings about a teacher's potential. Do not be offended if you are offered a lower rate than what you are accustomed to. Simply let the studio know your usual rate and ask how you can influence the pay rate they have offered. This should be the conversation opener. You may say: "Well, actually, I am used to a pay rate of $____ per class/hour. So, my question is how many students would I need to average, over what period of time, in order to earn this amount?" You may add: "I am willing to accept your offer, but with the opportunity to be re-evaluated at a later date once I've had the opportunity to build my class attendance. Would this be acceptable to you?" How a studio responds to your proposal will be very revealing to you.

> ❝❝ **Studios typically offer a lower starting pay to begin with until they get their bearings about a teacher's potential.**

Here are some possible responses and what they may tell you about the studio:

Response #1: "There is no room for negotiation."

What you've been offered is what they pay. My feeling on this is that you may be talking to a large corporation with numerous locations. The larger the company the less empowered management may be to adjust pay rates based on performance. However, these businesses may conduct periodic evaluations that may offer you an opportunity for a raise if your class is performing well. If this is the case, you might ask if and how often the studio conducts performance reviews. This does not mean you should decline the job outright. There may be other factors that make this employment opportunity attractive, especially if you are still building your resume. If the pay is low, but the prestige is high, accept one class on the schedule versus committing all your time to that studio.

Response #2: "Well, no one has ever asked us that. Let me get back with you."

Congratulations! You just set yourself apart from any other candidate and management just revealed something very important to you: how they respond to an unfamiliar situation. This would indicate to me that this studio operates thoughtfully and with an open mind. If you get a response like this, this studio is a keeper! I suspect they will get back to you with a well thought out answer and plan.

Response #3: "Of course! In order to earn $___ you will have to average ___ over ___ amount of time. How much time do you think you'll comfortably need to achieve this goal?"

This studio is on top of its game. They know their business. They think in terms of numbers as well as people. They understand the value of their teachers. My feeling here is that this studio would be a pleasure to teach for—as long as you stay on top of your game as well. Expect to be held accountable in meeting the expectations of your contract. Be very precise in your communication with this studio. Ask for a ninety day trial to start with. It may take you longer to establish your class, but as long as you know you are working toward whatever goal they give you, you should be able to remain motivated.

Response #4: "Um, ah, err, not sure what to tell you. We don't provide this information to teachers."

This is not a good sign. If you need the teaching experience, take the job but temper your expectations accordingly. It is highly unlikely you have much of a future with this studio (or they in business!).

You may hear one of these responses or none of them. These are simply a few possibilities. The point is that successful negotiation requires you to pay attention to what is being communicated to you. If a studio reveals they have no flexibility in their pay rate, it would be futile for you to continue to press them for a chance to increase your attendance in hopes for greater compensation. A studio that is not prepared for your question but requests time to get back to you, as well as a studio that immediately recognizes the value of what you are proposing, are both scenarios that indicate great potential; the conversation is not over. A studio that does not share attendance goals when requested by a teacher could prove to be troublesome down the road (if not out of the starting gate).

Teacher pay models typically fall into one of four categories:

1. A flat rate per class or per hour.
2. A "per head" amount (which is usually a few dollars per student), or a sliding scale based on attendance.
3. A flat rate plus bonus if certain attendance goals are met.
4. A percentage of the revenue generated by their class.

Each of these models has its pros and cons. Let's take a

closer look at each one:

A flat rate is great because it provides an expected level of income to the teacher which does not fluctuate according to attendance. The downside to a flat rate is that it doesn't automatically increase as your class builds in attendance.

The "per head," "sliding scale" or "bonus pay" models are structured to provide incentives and reward teachers for their marketing efforts. On the upside, the "pay per head" model works great if the studio has a large enough student base to support large numbers in each class. On the downside, new teachers may earn below the industry average until they are able to build their attendance (which can take months). This can create financial hardship for new talent breaking into the business. My suggestion is if you are confident in your ability to build a class quickly, and the studio has a large student population and a large classroom space to accommodate many students, you should consider this model if presented to you. The great thing about the "per head" model is that your marketing and community-building efforts are immediately rewarded.

The percentage of "class revenue" model is the least common of the four. As with the "per head" model, compensation is determined solely by attendance. This model is actually the most attractive for a studio because it ties teacher compensation directly to revenue and within a specified ratio. Unfortunately, studio software technology is unable to provide an accurate "real time" reading on class revenue due to the variety of pricing options offered at most studios. This model would work only if every student paid the exact amount for class each time they came. Very few studios operate under this business model.

A minimum pay guarantee with a "per head" model is most often considered the ideal. Attendance fluctuates and on the days when you may have only a few students in class, the minimum guarantee is a life saver. If a "per head fee" is proposed to you without a minimum guarantee, suggest a guarantee. Speak up. If you accept a pay structure that has the potential to cause you financial stress, this will affect you. Feel confident in bringing this up during your financial negotiations. Studios understand that stressed out teachers are not good for business. If they made you an offer, they want you. Now, it's just a question of working out an arrangement that is equitable for both parties. Never lose sight of the partnership aspect of your relationship with a studio.

The important thing to remember when negotiating your compensation is that in doing so, you demonstrate a deeper understanding and appreciation for the business you are in. This alone will impress the studio you are considering. Studios are always on the look-out for teaching talent. If a great talent approaches them who also understands the business side of their craft, I am very confident that studio would be absolutely delighted to speak frankly about attendance and compensation!

Thirty-four

"Ethics is knowing the difference between what you have
a right to do and what is right to do."
–Potter Stewart

Teaching at Various Competing
Studios: Build Your Empire Wisely

*T*eachers who derive 100 percent (or close) of their income
from teaching may elect to teach at various studios, unless
they find substantial employment with just one studio. There
definitely is a right and a wrong way to juggle collaboration with
multiple studios. The "right" way will open many doors for you.
The "wrong" way may slam those doors shut. Here is what you need
to know.

Many teaching contracts have a "non-compete" clause that
establishes that teaching at a studio within a specified radius (in
miles) is not permitted. If you are teaching at studios that are close
enough to each other so that students are willing to drive to both
(or all) locations, be careful because you may end up "cannibalizing"
your student base. This means that it may weaken your attendance

at any given studio which in turn will negatively affect your ability to negotiate a higher pay rate. Spreading your student followers across multiple studios may also interfere with the formation of community in your classes at any given studio. Even the most dedicated of students will only take so many classes a week. There is a limit to what their bodies can withstand, or their financial situations can support.

> " **You are the same wonderful teacher wherever you teach. But perception, even if inaccurate, can dictate your perceived financial worth.**

Furthermore, your attractiveness to a studio may likely diminish if the owner/manager becomes aware of the proximity of your other classes. Again, if you consider your relationship with a studio to be a partnership, management will surely not be happy if they are worried you may be unintentionally siphoning students from their customer base for the benefit of a competitor. Even if this is not your intent, you cannot control the preferences of your students. They are free to go wherever they like and if they are following you from studio to studio, asking them not to do this is an awkward conversation! So again, pay close attention to the content of the "non-compete clause". A contract violation of this nature could cost you a valuable relationship.

Here are some rules for professional conduct that will lead to long lasting and successful (multiple) competing studio relationships:

- **Rule 1:** Make sure your studios are far apart and that you are not in violation of any non-compete restrictions.
- **Rule 2:** Make sure all the studios where you teach are on a comparable pricing model.

Teachers who teach at an upscale studio that charges more for their classes (likely because the overhead on an upscale studio is naturally higher) and also teach at a lower scale studio that charges less, are sending a message to their students. Students will compare pricing. Studios that charge less for your classes can diminish the value of your classes at the upscale one.

Let's say the upscale studio invests in the branding of your classes and your superior teaching ability; they are marketing you as a cut above. If students then discover they can take your superior classes for less money at another studio, the end result does not bode well for the studio that made the investment in you. You are not likely to be paid higher at a studio that charges less for your class, so there's that too. Not only would you be putting into jeopardy your relationship with the nicer studio, you might also be paid less to do so.

In the world of business, it all boils down to optics. You are the same wonderful teacher wherever you teach. But perception, even if inaccurate, can dictate your perceived financial worth. It's not fair to you. You are trying to make a living. You teach a great class. You love your students. Why should you have to concern yourself with studio politics? I've known a number of teachers who have taken this position—with an unfortunate outcome. Indeed, you are an excellent teacher, but you can't exist in a bubble and be successful. Be mindful of the business aspect of the studios where you teach. If your class is valued at $25 to drop in at one studio, please think twice before you teach at a studio that offers your class experience for $15. It's sends a conflicting message to your students. Is your class experience worth $25 or $15? Which amount reflects your real worth? Be consistent; it brings credibility to your value as a teacher.

- **Rule 3:** When marketing your classes on social media, do so individually by studio.

Sweeping notifications that include everywhere you teach dilute your message. Market your classes individually by studio so you can really hone in on that particular class experience and community. On social media, each studio where you teach should have its own dedicated post. If you teach several classes at the same studio and want to post a general notification, by all means list them. Otherwise, posting individually about your classes gives you more reasons to post regularly.

If you have a professional website, it's a good idea to list all your classes and studios there. A website is passive marketing; social media is active. Your website is where prospective studios and students will go to learn about you. It's information waiting to be found (and therefore passive). Social media is active in that your message gets broadcast to people in your network. A social media post is typically a call to action. In advertising, an effective call to action is simple, singular and direct. Too many options, (take my class here and here and here!) may overwhelm.

In conclusion: Be mindful of where you choose to teach! Make sure each competing studio is far apart, on comparable pricing models and market them separately!

Thirty-five

"Marketing is enthusiasm transferred to the customer."
–Gregory Ciotti

Marketing and Managing Your Class Successfully: Get the Word Out

A few years ago, I hired a teacher to take over a very successful class. The original teacher was moving away and recommended this particular teacher as a good replacement. He felt his students would embrace this person and the class would be able to continue. We arranged for an audition and made the usual announcement, created a beautiful banner image for marketing, wrote an enticing class description and blasted the news about this great new class and teacher on all our channels. The class debuted to twenty eager students and we were ecstatic to have been so fortunate to find such a suitable teacher to carry on this wonderful class!

The following week rolled around and instead of twenty

students, he had nine people in attendance. The following week he had eight, then six, then three, then no one, then again three, then no-one. This pattern continued for another month with the class alternating between no one and only a handful of students showing up. It takes time for a class to gel, and the journey is typically up and down until it does. However, the attendance in this class took a significant drop and never recovered. It became apparent that the class was in a downward spiral and needed attention.

I reached out to the teacher to talk to him about it. I asked for his thoughts on his declining attendance. He told me he had no idea why students weren't returning. Then I inquired about his marketing, if he had announced his class on his social media, and how was he spreading the word. He gave me a puzzled look and said: "What do you mean? I don't use my social media for business. Marketing my class is your job, not mine. My job is to teach."

{ **A teacher's relationship with the studio is one of partnership. Classes are built from two marketing perspectives, not just one.** }

Studio management can blast out how much they love a particular class, how much they are excited to have a specific teacher on the schedule and how great his/her class is. But it also takes the teacher to communicate his/her enthusiasm to be teaching at that studio and how much he/she appreciates the students attending. Both points of view must be expressed, because they give credibility to each other. A studio that doesn't brag about his/her teachers gives the impression there is nothing to brag about and teachers who don't brag about their studio and the classes they teach also give the impression there's nothing special there, either. It is so important that both parties contribute to the marketing aspect of the business. Do your part in marketing your class and your studio should do its part.

Privately owned studios tend to give greater creative reign over teacher marketing, especially if the teacher is on salary as a full-time employee. Whereas corporate studios or franchises with multiple locations may have stricter marketing policies, smaller studios may respond to a teacher's marketing efforts with greater support for his/her creative ideas. The best rule of thumb is to always inquire about boundaries. If the studio has a marketing plan in place which is not open to a teacher's marketing efforts, then really, all the teacher has to do is focus on delivering a great class experience. Otherwise, your studio is likely to expect some degree of marketing from you.

Marketing is the act of creating demand, or tapping into an existing demand, for a product or service. Advertising is a component of marketing that focuses more on a "call to action" which is typically linked to a sale. Marketing your class doesn't mean you should buy an ad in a publication or purchase air time on the radio. There are several ways to market your class that don't require a financial investment, or a great deal of time. Here are a few things you can and should do:

1. Are you happy to be teaching? Let the world know. Tell all your friends. Tell everybody! It doesn't matter if they can come to your class or not. Let people know what you are doing. When I opened dance 101 in 2004, I used my cell phone as the studio phone so I would never miss a call. I carried class schedules in my purse and gave them out everywhere I went—in the check-out line at the grocery store, at neighboring businesses, on the cars parked around me (which is now illegal—don't do this!), etc. Every day I committed to giving out ten schedules. Sometimes it would take me as little as ten to fifteen minutes and on other days, longer. I once handed a schedule to a lady I passed at the

mall because she looked like a dancer (and she was!). I will never know how many of these schedules actually attracted a student to the studio. But I do remember a lovely woman who said she found our schedule on the pavement as she was walking to her car. It may have blown off a car or been tossed, but she found it and considered it an omen. She grew up dancing and missed it terribly. Every person you tell about your classes is like a pebble dropped into a pond. You may not know how far the ripples may reach, but they will travel. Who you tell may not come to class, but they may tell someone who will. Or they may come and bring a friend.

2. Social media has made it easier than ever to let people know what we're up to. Many teachers create a Facebook business or "group" page for their classes. Students can easily search for the page and opt in. Teachers can upload class photos, class playlists, make announcements, post videos (be careful about using copyrighted music), share recipes, share articles, etc. A well managed page with continuous fresh content also helps to keep students engaged. They can share experiences, comment on photos and remain connected to their classmates long after the class has ended. This dialog creates community among students (more on this in Chapter 35 and 36). Instagram is also a very popular tool. Teachers who post regularly on this medium can amass a large number of followers and in the process their account can become a resume of sorts. A well managed social media presence will attract students as well as potential employers. We've hired teachers whose work we've admired on Instagram.

3. Develop an online presence. Create a website! Post your bio, resume, pictures, videos, student testimonials, and list the

classes you teach and where. Write a blog! A well written and researched blog can add credibility to your expertise and gives you the opportunity to express your personality and your love for what you do. Your website is also a convenient way for students to see where and when you're teaching. When we receive a teaching inquiry, we always look to see if the teacher has a website. A professional looking site can also help you land a coveted position with a good studio.

4. Word of mouth is, hands down, the most effective marketing and advertising tool out there. Ask your students to invite a friend to class. If your studio allows you to comp new students into your class, offer to comp your students' friends into your classes on their first visit. Engage your students in the success of the class. Ask them to help you build a beautiful community of like minded individuals.

5. Familiarize yourself with your studio's class packages and memberships. If asked, you should be able to answer questions about new student specials or the cost to drop in. The more you know about the business side of your class and the studio where you teach, the more enthusiastic and professional you appear.

6. Seek out opportunities to teach your class outside the studio. Offer a free class at your neighborhood park. Participate in community events and fundraisers where you teach in exchange for donations to a cause. These opportunities not only enable you to give of yourself, but are also a great way for people to experience what you do.

7. Do you have an idea for a specialty class? A holiday themed class, a costume themed class, a retro class, a donation class

for a cause, bring your kids to class day, or prenatal barre, etc.? Pitch it to your studio! If it is something they can get behind, they'll help you promote it. Studios love to have news to share. If you've got an idea for something fun, chances are your studio will jump all over it and you will give them a reason to advertise, promote and hype your class and you as a teacher! And if you're having a wonderful class . . . pull out your phone when/if appropriate and film a piece of it! Post the video and tag your students, or AirDrop it to them at the end of class. Be sure to ask your students' permission before you post!

The point is to get the word out and to remain in the awareness of your students. Use your imagination! But always clear it with your studio. I cannot stress this enough. You must involve your studio because you are partners. If the management doesn't support your idea, either come up with a new one or ask if you can do it but not mention the studio.

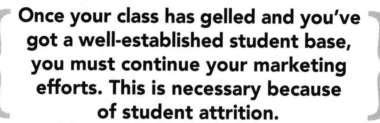

Once your class has gelled and you've got a well-established student base, you must continue your marketing efforts. This is necessary because of student attrition.

Even your most enthusiastic regulars may not be with you for long. Life is a journey in motion. Students get married, divorced, have kids, change jobs or careers, move away, develop a new interest, are caring for a sick relative, suffer an injury . . . any number of things may cause you to lose a student. Teachers who sit back once they've hit their magic number of students, will watch that number dwindle over time. You should always be working on attracting and retaining new students. Make marketing a permanent part of your work week by setting aside time for it.

Whether you are an active participant in the marketing of your class, or simply only required to teach, growth is the oxygen of your class. You must be seeing new faces every week to cement the future of your class. Your studio is in the same position. Together as partners, a studio and its teachers must be continuously engaged in marketing. Whether jointly or separately, this is a necessity for the creation of a win-win-win (studio, teacher, and student) outcome.

Thirty-six

"Individually, we are one drop. Together, we are an ocean."
–Ryunosuke Satoro

Building a Community

A few days ago I was able to catch up with dance 101 rockstar teacher Ashleigh H. I was laying the groundwork for this chapter and wanted to talk to her about the community she has built around her dance 101 classes.

Ashleigh could be the poster child for much of what I've written in this book. She is, in my opinion, one of the finest teachers I've ever had the pleasure to work with and a great example of an exceptional community builder. Ashleigh teaches dance fitness and body sculpt classes called Reb3l Groove and Reb3l Strength respectively. She debuted on our schedule in March of 2017 with eleven students in her dance fitness class. Her attendance grew each week, from eleven to thirteen to eighteen to nineteen to twentyone.

In her fifth week of teaching, her class had grown to thirty-one students. Six months into teaching, her Saturday class now averages forty students and growing. This is the ideal growth trajectory for a class.

Over the course of the last fourteen years, dance 101 has never witnessed a teacher grow her classes so quickly. Truthfully, this process can take years! I see Ashleigh's attendance every week and I am amazed. Her content is great and her presentation is awesome—but that is not unique to her. We have many highly trained, professional, talented and personable teachers whose classes are not as well attended. What does Ashleigh do differently?

> ❝ **Ashleigh's approach to her class is a great example of how excellence is in the details.**

When Ashleigh crossed over from student to teacher, she brought with her a deep appreciation for how dance fitness had impacted her life. She had previously given birth to two beautiful boys and had some stubborn baby weight to lose. She had always loved to dance, had natural rhythm and a good ear for music. Feeling a bit confined in her role as a mother (as many of us do), she was delighted to discover how her dance classes made her feel youthful and carefree. As she watched her body return to her pre-pregnancy weight, she increasingly felt better about herself.

Those classes opened a portal for her. They provided a momentary escape in which she was able to focus on herself. It was her "me time". As she slimmed down she went shopping for new, smaller sized outfits to wear to class. She loved seeing the changes in her body, becoming more comfortable with her image in the studio mirror as she moved to the music. She delighted in the community of friends she had made. The expectation of seeing them in class and grabbing a coffee afterwards helped motivate her on days when she felt her life was too hectic to release her for an hour to herself. She remembered the excitement of walking into class—knowing she was about to do something healthy, fun and exciting along with other rockstar dancers. Over time, she grew increasingly adept at executing and remembering choreography. Before long she was asked to sub classes, eventually landing a class of her own. When Ashleigh became a teacher she remembered all these aspects of her experience and set about creating the same kind of environment for her students. And they responded—in droves.

Ashleigh's approach to her class is a great example of how excellence is in the details. She sets the stage for her class experience by arriving early and turning on her music—to set the tone. As students begin arriving, they walk into a sound cloud of upbeat music. She greets everyone and welcomes them to the class, making a mental

> **When Ashleigh crossed over from student to teacher, she brought with her a deep appreciation for how dance fitness had impacted her life.**

note of who is new and where they are standing in the class so she can keep an eye on them. She often will introduce a new student to a regular who echoes her great enthusiasm and will encourage them about "how we all look like a fool for our first five classes or so, and to stick with it because it does get easier" she says. After class she will approach new students with words of encouragement, inviting them to return. She will invite them to join the class social media group with the hope they will be drawn into their supportive and friendly circle, helping them to feel included. When you step into Ashleigh's class, you are stepping into a welcoming community of new friends yet to be made.

Ashleigh commands her classroom. Everything about her exudes confidence and purpose. She is always "dressed" in cool gear—

> **There's content and there's community: two separate aspects of a successful class that must be inclusive.**

with her ripped leggings, belt, crop top, Adidas high tops and a flannel shirt tied around her waist exposing her impressive mid-section. She wears her hair in braids or two top knots and sometimes loose and flowing under her skull cap. There's a loud subtlety to her fashion sense. I always look forward to seeing what she's wearing and laugh when she recounts the remarks her husband makes when he sees her as she leaves the house (Is it Halloween today?). She has a unique fashion sense that adds a cool factor that she is an example of—and it's contagious. Over time I've watched many of her students transform from frumpy sweats and T-shirts to looking like music video back-up dancers. It's quite exciting, actually, and it makes sense. "You're staring at yourself in the mirror and you want to feel good about yourself. I add a fashion spin to my class and students love it. They get dressed up to take class and that makes it more fun—like a night out" she says.

Class fashion and community are expressed in selfies and group shots posted onto the class social media page. Ashleigh will post healthy, low calorie recipes, class reminders and announcements, often commenting and engaging with whoever posts on the page. Students begin "friending" each other and the community deepens. All the while Ashleigh is front and center as the community's commander-in-chief and gratitude for her abounds. Students arrived thirty minutes early on her birthday to decorate the classroom with streamers, balloons and Happy Birthday banners. Someone made a cheese cake (Ashleigh's favorite) and others arrived with gifts.

There's content and there's community: two separate aspects of a successful class that must be inclusive. Sure, Ashleigh teaches a really fun class that will get you in great shape. But what makes the class mega successful is not only its objective, but also the life impacting sense of belonging, support, and community that each student experiences. A successful class has to fire on all cylinders: great content, excellent delivery, inspiring music, marketing, and community. Combined, these elements not only create an experience that is productive (produces results) but also satisfies our need for connection. People want things they need but they also want things that matter.

> " **People want things they need but they also want things that matter.**

When I think about marketing and community building, I am often reminded of the saying: "If a tree falls in the forest and no one is around to hear it, does it make a sound?" If you have a wonderful product and nobody knows about it, does it exist? Of course it does! And yes the tree makes a sound, but **only awareness can validate the existence of anything.** Marketing will get the word out, but community building is what motivates students to return and keep returning. Apply these two strategies and you virtually guarantee the success of your class (and a huge circle of friends, too).

Thirty-seven

"If it happens once, it may never happen again.
But if it happens twice it's a pattern
and will happen again."
–Paulo Coelho

Subs and Cancellations

I have not been able to find any empirical evidence to support what I'm about to tell you. My knowledge on this subject is purely anecdotal. Over the course of my career, I've observed students become very attached to their fitness instructors and teachers. There are two theories about how long it takes for a habit to form. For many years the conventional wisdom was twenty-one days, but more recent studies propose a longer period of sixty-six days. Either way, once you become established as a teacher and your classes have been on a consistent schedule for a few months, you will most likely have built a community of regulars. Your "tribe" will form and whereas these students may have been initially attracted by your class content, what may keep them returning is your personality and who you are as a person and motivator. It may be something as simple as your smile and your attitude, the music you play, or it may be the results they've experienced because of your teaching methods. It could be all of these reasons or it could be something else which is very personal to them! Regardless of the "why", a community will develop in your classes over time, and along with this relationship, regular students develop an emotional attachment. When your students think about attending your class, an image of you comes to mind. They "see" you and they "see" images of the other students (their friends), who they hope to see when attending. They may also visualize the classroom, remember a song you play and picture themselves in the class. These mental images will motivate your students to look forward to your class. Imagine what happens when they show up and you're not there. Disappointment! Good-naturedly, some may shrug it off and be open to a new experience. Others may sulk throughout the class; and others may simply turn around and leave. Occasionally, students may complain to the front desk (which is never pleasant), but since the teacher is not present to witness it, many have absolutely no idea how their absences affect their students. For this reason, I am really happy you are reading this chapter!

Your absences are manageable. The solution is not impeccable attendance (although that would be awesome, it's not realistic). You will have absences. It's an eventuality that everyone expects. Nobody is a machine. You need a vacation every so often. You need to take care of yourself if you're sick or not feeling well. You may have a family commitment, or you've traveled home for the holidays. Flat tire, car trouble, etc. Life happens! Your studio understands this. Your students

> **When your students think about attending your class, an image of you comes to mind.**

understand this. The issue is not whether you'll miss a class here and there; the issue is how it is handled.

Some studios will locate and schedule subs for you. However, if you are responsible for securing your own subs, the following is written for you. Please consider these guidelines for identifying, recruiting, developing and managing your subs.

The Ten Golden Rules about Subs and Cancellations

Rule 1
No subs or cancellations during the first ninety days after debuting a class.

This is the only period of time when you absolutely cannot miss a class unless it's an emergency (and careful how you define "emergency"). Those first ninety days are critical for your community to form. Students will be talking about your class and making recommendations to their friends. There'll be a buzz around the studio and it takes time for the word to spread. Some people may have to rearrange their schedule to be able to attend and may not make it in for a few weeks. Opinions will be forming about you and your class content. This is a vulnerable time for your class and if you are absent, word may circulate that you may not be reliable or that you're not committed to your class. When a studio offers you the opportunity to teach, do not commit to it until you've checked your calendar and are reasonably sure you will not miss a class during the first ninety days. Your studio would prefer to postpone your debut than to sabotage its success with an expected absence during this critical period.

We recently hired a phenomenally talented teacher who came highly recommended. Her credits were off the charts; she was very pleasant and presented herself very professionally. There was no need to audition her. We had already seen her work and on the basis of this knowledge, we offered her a very nice compensation package and gave her two prime time class slots on the Saturday schedule.

> **"There is no subbing a class that hasn't yet gelled... Students will not support it!**

The marketing arm of the studio kicked into gear, writing her class descriptions and branding her concept. Her debut was heavily promoted via e-mail, on our blog, social media and word of mouth to key students (influencers). We created a huge amount of hype around this teacher's arrival, barely able to contain our excitement about what our students were about to experience in her classes! For a solid week, it was all we could talk about! Saturday arrived and many students came out to welcome her onto the schedule. They loved the class and thought she was pretty amazing. She was off and running! We were sure, in a matter of weeks, her classes would be monster packed and we would be raising her pay. It was a slam dunk, win-win-win for the studio, the teacher and the students. Monday rolls around (two days later) and I get an email: "Oh, by the way, I forgot to tell you I'll be out next weekend and can't teach. Can you get me a sub?" My heart sank, and I remember thinking to myself: "She just threw her class away (and our efforts to launch her). She sabotaged the opportunity we had given her and put us (the studio) into a difficult position." Rule 1 emphasizes: There is no subbing a class that hasn't yet gelled . . . Students will not support it!

Rule 2
Cultivate your subs. Not just anyone will do.

Be sure your subs are qualified, are familiar with your content and can deliver a great class. The ideal scenario is that your subs have attended your class and even better, if they are your top students (who you have trained). Your students will likely champion them and the community remains intact without the introduction of an "outsider" to lead the experience. This may not be possible because you may not have ideal candidates. But, if you do, you should cultivate them.

Other great sub candidates would be fellow teachers with whom you share students. Ideally, you will have taken their class to experience their teaching style and find it to be a good fit for your students. Familiarity is a definite plus when it comes to subs, and this also gives your sub an opportunity to promote their own classes. This is also a great reason for you to sub for others as you would be able to promote your classes to their students as well.

Less desirable subs, even if they are hugely qualified, are those from outside the studio culture. Many students are reticent about taking a class from someone they don't know. However, if it goes well, the next time the same one subs for you, he or she will be a familiar face and thus more likely to be well received.

> **The worst possible sub scenario (to be avoided at all costs) is someone who is unfamiliar with your class, not at your level of training and unknown to your students.**

These subs can't possibly even come close to replicating your content—in any regard. If this is the only sub scenario available to you in a pinch, it might be better to cancel your class and ask the studio to announce a special "Pop-Up" class with this sub as a guest teacher in your time slot.

Rule 3
If you don't have a great sub, it's better to cancel the class.

Bad subs will damage a class, ruin the momentum of your success and harm your students' confidence in your ability to secure a good sub for them. It can also be a bad reflection on the studio who may be blamed for the sub. Some students may react aggressively, although this is more the exception than the rule. I once received an anonymous e-mail from a group of students who complained that a particular sub they experienced was "an insult to the class". By any account, that was a harsh reaction and a very bold statement. Please understand that students take your subs personally. They may feel slighted and disregarded when a sub isn't up to par.

Rule 4
Three consecutive absences will "kill" a class.

Three is the magic number. We've seen this happen many times; it may just as well qualify as empirical evidence. In the words of the great philosopher and author, Paulo Coelho, as quoted in his famous book *The Alchemist*: "*If it happens once, it may never happen again. But if it happens twice it's a pattern and will happen again.*" I believe we all know this at an intrinsic level, even if we are unfamiliar with this quote. Once may not happen again. Twice is a pattern and the third time confirms the pattern. In this scenario, the quality of your subs is not relevant, they are a temporary place holder. Multiple consecutive subs cannot "carry" a class; it loses its direction. And if you have the same sub for all three classes, that class now belongs to the sub. This pattern relates to the adult fitness market. As you'll hear me say often: "Students are loyal, but fickle". Adults will move on if they feel a teacher has abandoned their class, and this typically happens after the third consecutive cancellation, because a pattern has emerged.

Rule 5
Secure your own subs.

No one knows your class experience better than you. Unless studio management is very familiar with your class, he/she couldn't possibly know who would make a great sub for you. You are the most qualified person to select an appropriate sub for your class. If you pass this responsibility to others who are not familiar with your class, you are taking a big risk. Remember, the wrong sub can harm your class attendance and you'll notice it as soon as the following week. Some students might not return until they know for sure you are back, and this may take time!

Rule 6
"Sell" your sub!

When you know you'll be out, it would be a professional gesture for you to announce your sub when you inform your class that you'll be absent. Do it with enthusiasm! Tell your students about your sub and why you are excited for them to have this new experience. You may want to share a bit of information about your sub's training and his /her qualifications if you know your students are not familiar with him/her. Or if your sub teaches at the studio, you may reference his/ her classes. Excitement is contagious. If your students perceive your excitement about the sub, they will feel it too. This does not guarantee your students will attend the class, but it surely helps.

Rule 7
Ask your students for feedback about your sub
and listen to what they say!

What did they think about the sub? Did they enjoy the class? Would they like to have the sub teach the class again? What constructive feedback can they give about how the sub taught the class? Be proactive. Your students may not give you any feedback unless you ask for it; especially if they didn't care for the sub. Most students would rather not say anything negative— unless you specifically ask. You can tell your students that their feedback would be helpful to you, because you want to make sure they are taken care of and this requires their input. Maybe the warm-up was too long or the cool down wasn't what they were expecting. Maybe the class moved too quickly or too slowly. These are things you can relate to your sub without hurting any feelings. If your students tell you they just didn't like the sub, well, that you can keep to yourself and try another sub. You can't change an individual's personality. If it's not a good fit, move on. When you involve your students in this way, it sends a message that you respect and honor the class experience they are expecting. It acknowledges them and conveys your appreciation for them. It's always a good tact to inquire about your sub's performance. You'll get useful information and your students will feel like they have a voice. If your students feel like they have a voice in your class, they'll feel a greater sense of ownership and from this, a greater level of loyalty and consistent attendance will emerge.

Rule 8
If your sub is late or a no-show, understand the consequences!

I don't think I need to elaborate too much here. Your sub is a reflection on you. If this happens, all you can do is apologize! Even if your sub's late arrival or no-show was because of something legitimate that might have happened, the experience will have left a bad impression on your students that you cannot undo. You can go into all sorts of explanation, but the next time you schedule that sub, your students will be skeptical and may not show.

Rule 9
If you know (at least one week in advance) that you will be out, and you do not have a high quality sub on deck, ask your studio management for guidance.

With many studios now using apps, class cancellations are visible to the public and can be communicated in time to reach your regulars. I can't speak for other studios, but dance 101 would prefer to cancel a class than offer a "less than" experience to its members.

Rule 10
**Last minute cancellations are class killers.
Avoid like the plague.**

Do everything possible to teach your classes. They are fragile in this sense. Students can be extremely loyal and fickle at the same time (there, I said it again!). It doesn't take much to develop a reputation for last minute cancellations and if you do, it will adversely affect your class attendance. If your students are not confident that you will make it to class, they aren't going to risk the drive across town. I've seen many great classes decline or "die" as a result of this. The same applies to tardiness. Teachers who are consistently late will also harm their classes—no matter how talented or wonderful they may be.

How your absences are managed will directly impact the long term success of your classes—for better or for worse. The best way to develop a network of viable subs is to begin cultivating them from day one. You will eventually need a sub. Do not wait until the last minute to find one. Get to know the other teachers at your studio. Take their classes. Develop a list of your preferred go-to subs so you know who to call when the time comes. Offer to sub for them as well. In studio culture, teachers who sub for others have little problem finding subs for their own classes. Pay it forward!

You should also be aware of how your absences affect your studio. A cancelled class causes your studio to suffer a financial loss. A poorly placed sub causes even greater financial loss because, in addition to the potential lack of attendance, the studio must also pay the sub. On the flip side, subs can present a great opportunity for your studio to scout new talent. Most teachers get their start by subbing. It's a great way to break into the business and get noticed by the studio management.

Plan ahead for your absences! Develop a sub-network and follow "The Ten Golden Rules About Subs and Cancellations"! It will give you great peace of mind knowing that your students are taken care of while you're out; and your studio will be very appreciative of your professionalism.

> **In studio culture, teachers who sub for others have little problem finding subs for their own classes. Pay it forward!**

Thirty-eight

"There's a trick to the 'graceful exit.' It begins with the vision to recognize when a job, a life stage, or a relationship is over—and let it go. It means leaving what's over without denying its validity or its past importance to our lives. It involves a sense of future, a belief that every exit line is an entry, that we are moving up, rather than out."

–Ellen Goodman

Exiting a Studio Professionally

*I*f you have yet to break into this business, I wonder if you might be scratching your head pondering why I've dedicated a chapter to this topic. You might think: "Well, obviously, one should never leave any job on bad terms, no matter what job it is, nor the circumstances"—and you are right about that. But in this industry, that can be a lot easier said than done. There is a celebrity facet of teaching that sets it apart from other professions. Successful teachers live in the public eye.

A teacher's departure may affect hundreds of people who will no longer be enjoying class together. News will travel fast, far and wide. This is because teachers in the boutique fitness industry build communities. Relationships are formed that often lead to deep, loving friendships—not only between students, but also between the teacher and his or her students. Students become attached to their teachers and may feel a deep sense of loss and concern for their teacher's well-being.

> **Exiting a studio has a deeper impact than simply leaving a job. Students lives are affected and that's what makes it so newsworthy.**

If it is your decision to leave a studio, it can be very easy to exit gracefully. You make an announcement thanking the studio for the opportunity and when asked you share news about your next move. But what happens if there's a disagreement, or a conflict, or a directional change in management that no longer renders your relationship with the studio to be viable or simply not a good fit any longer? What then? If you were to quit, or were let go from, a corporate job, only a small number of people might be aware of it—like your bosses and coworkers. But if you are a popular teacher at a high profile studio, your departure may be big news among the many people who can no longer take their favorite class with you there. The ensuing number of eyeballs on you and the subsequent pressure from inquiries about why you are leaving may be overwhelming if you don't prepare in advance to deal with the situation. If the announcement is made on social media, it can potentially reach thousands of followers. That's a lot of people who will be curious about why their favorite teacher is leaving their studio.

In general, how any teacher (and studio) responds to this kind of attention could potentially be disastrous on both sides— or it can slip by with relatively little attention and in a positive light (which is the ideal for both parties). To diffuse a potentially uncomfortable situation, I highly recommend both teacher and studio set aside their grievances to prepare in advance and formulate a genuine neutral response that will keep everyone's reputation intact, demonstrating a high level of professionalism on both sides. On the teacher's behalf, it is essential that a teacher's explanation, whether in a social situation or as a message on social media, does not place blame on anyone. The same applies to the studio. Blaming only creates drama, invites more questions, and the situation can quickly spiral out of control. Here's the thing about blame: it's toxic for everyone.

A teacher who disparages a former studio may tarnish his/ her reputation in the industry (industry meaning potential studio employers and students alike). Conversely, a studio who disparages a former teacher does the same (who'd want to work for a studio that conducts itself in this way?). There are no winners in the blame game. My best advice is to tread carefully. Former teachers should not blame and should not gossip. They should move on. If a teacher lashes out publicly about a former studio, it places the studio in an uncomfortable situation in which it may feel obligated to respond in some way. Negative publicity is something all studios wish to avoid and if the management team is mature, they may likely remain neutral (even when under attack) because they may believe it is the only dignified course of action. However, if studio management is poor and chooses to respond in kind, the situation can escalate a hundred fold, wreaking havoc on everybody's reputation: teacher and studio alike. If you feel you've been dealt an unfair hand, do whatever you can to hold your anger in check, request a letter of recommendation, thank the studio for the opportunity, shake hands and exit. Do not lose sight of the bigger picture. A studio that has disparaged you publicly will feel the consequences of their decision to do so. You don't need to lash back. It's overkill. And if you are the one who is speaking ill of your former studio, you also will feel the consequences (which can be damaging to your career).

Since dance 101 opened in 2004, I have witnessed many teachers come and go. I often tell people that the door to dance 101 is a revolving one with most every one of our teachers returning at some time or another. Chances are greatly in your favor that you may never experience a disastrous exit. However, I am including this chapter because the consequences of such an exit are simply too severe not to give you a heads up. I have personally witnessed the devastating blow of a mangled studio exit on a teacher's career and it is heartbreaking. By their own hand, teachers who lash out publicly about their former studio may alienate other teachers at that studio who feel the sting of their negative comments. They may establish themselves in the industry as someone not to hire. They may also lose a number of students who they're angered along the way. Students who love their studio may not enjoy hearing it be throttled. It is an extremely sad thing to watch happen—especially knowing it could have and should have been avoided. I don't want this ever to happen to you.

> **If you feel you've been dealt an unfair hand, do whatever you can to hold your anger in check, request a letter of recommendation, thank the studio for the opportunity, shake hands and exit.**

When a studio exit is imminent, there are two things you should consider:

1. How you are going to handle it and . . .
2. How you choose to interpret it

As mentioned previously, the best way to handle a studio exit is to prepare a neutral response and stick to it. Crafting a credible response requires the author to believe it. This in turn, may require a little paradigm shift. You might want to dog-ear this page in case you ever find yourself on the uneasy brink of severing a studio relationship that is in conflict and no longer serving you.

Navigating a clean break will require you to recognize the catalyst for what it is: a tap on your shoulder to put your blinker on because you are about to make a turn. Whatever caused the catalyst is secondary to its appearance. A new direction in studio management, a manager or co-worker you don't like, an action taken that you don't understand, the consequences of poor attendance, a better offer at another studio, etc. may be what fuels the catalyst in your mind. But the real catalyst is your realization that it's time to make a change.

Whatever the catalyst, the universe has decided you need to move on. This is my personal perspective, by the way. I also believe that the more deeply we are entrenched in a situation (like really loving our job) the greater the jolt the universe delivers to set us in a new direction. I have no scientific data to support this—just a lot of years on this planet and a good many examples. When you see the writing on the wall and you know it's time to go, you must believe this change is necessary in order for the next great opportunity to show up for you. Give your notice or respect the notice given to you.

> " **Navigating a clean break will require you to recognize the catalyst for what it is: a tap on your shoulder to put your blinker on because you are about to make a turn.**

Ask for your letter of recommendation and exit professionally and gracefully. Wonderful, new experiences await you.

Before you go off thinking I must be living in La La land, let me assure you I've experienced many catalysts in my life that have uprooted me from the path I was on and onto another. In fact, I've had so many of these, when I announced to my kids that I was going to write a book, they automatically thought it was going to be on this subject! I've had the rug pulled out from underneath me and landed on my feet so many times, that I developed a philosophy about it. Try not to be angry, feel slighted or underappreciated. Instead, become curious about what's around the corner. Be positive! My torn ACL led to the development of my stretch class 17 years ago (that I still teach today). The most emotionally painful break-up I've ever experienced led me down a path of self-discovery. The list goes on. But it all boils down to this:

> **If you believe the universe conspires for your fulfillment, you will accept that all the directional changes and course corrections that show up are for your betterment—regardless of the short-term fallout.**

Try to let go of the unnecessary explaining "what happened was..., he said, she said" and embrace the "what's next".

Leaving a studio on good terms, with a letter of recommendation in hand only furthers you. The more doors you leave open during your career, the more opportunities you will have.

The studio you are about to leave should be a stepping stone on your journey. Exit with professionalism, dignity and integrity.

PART 4
Self-Care: Teaching for the Long Run

Thirty-nine

"If you don't take care of your body,
your body won't take care of you."
-BUBGreat

Self-Care is Not a Luxury

I admit it. I have a history of putting myself at the bottom of my list of priorities. I've pushed my body beyond healthy limits, fueled it poorly (out of ignorance), ignored warning signs of impending injury (hello torn ACL), and bitten my nails to the quick and twirled my hair into knots as my strategy for stress management. Until I was finally able to pull myself together and develop a daily habit of self care, I journeyed through life hanging on by a thread, praying not to get injured and that my stress level would disappear on its own. That's no way to live. Furthermore, it's a terrible strategy for longevity! I truly believe had I not turned myself around when I did, I doubt I'd currently be teaching as many classes a week as I still do at my age.

The moment you picked up this book, read the first chapter and turned the page, you embarked upon a journey toward exceptional teaching. But, all is for naught if you crash and burn early on. You are precious. As a teacher, you bring beauty into this world. You matter and you are needed. Self-care is not a luxury. It is a necessity.

> **" Longevity in our profession depends greatly on how we take care of ourselves today.**

Longevity in our profession depends greatly on how we take care of ourselves today. Longevity isn't automatic and it's certainly not a guarantee just because we are in great physical shape right now. Stamina requires fuel and mind health requires intention.

Crafting a great class, applying solid teaching strategies, engineering an exceptional experience, and creating a welcoming environment for our students are things we do in the present. However, longevity has to do with the future. To extend your career for as long as it fulfills you, steps must be taken from the very start to incorporate daily habits of self care.

Your body, your mind, and your overall spirit of well-being will reciprocate with vitality, clarity, and harmony!

There are three main areas of self-care: the body (nutrition and physical care), the mind (clarity of thoughts), and well-being (feeling in harmony and at peace). Teaching makes demands on all of them. We, as teachers, must be physically strong and able, we must properly fuel the physical aspect of our profession and we must be healthy and rested in mind and spirit in order to hold space for, and be patient with others. These aspects of our being can and do deplete as the day wears on. The body naturally recharges energy with rest and sleep, but nutrition and mind care are choices we make.

Unlike the consequences of lack of sleep, which can be

felt immediately, poor nutrition and lack of mind care can slowly compound over time into a greater problem that cannot be resolved over the course of one night. Proper nutrition and mind care should be daily practices that need to be incorporated into our work schedule.

Teaching class is only one aspect of this profession. Just as we must set aside time (outside of class) to mine for great music, update our class playlists, create choreography or sequencing, and attend to our social media marketing, we should also incorporate time into our busy schedule to prepare our meals and "clear out" our mind clutter. Our diet must provide us with the right amount of protein, fats and carbohydrates to support a high activity level and a healthy mind requires a daily regiment

  ** Proper nutrition and mind care should be daily practices that need to be incorporated into our work schedule.**

of energetic recovery. This book would not be complete without addressing these aspects of our teaching profession which also have a direct impact on our life in general. Yes, they are that important.

The following chapters are not intended to disperse medical, nutritional nor spiritual advice. I am only sharing with you the information I have gathered on my personal journey to self-care. In sharing my story, I hope it sparks your own journey to find what works for you. We each need different things. These chapters on self-care outline what has (and is) working for me. This is the story of my personal journey to develop a lifelong strategy that enables me to dance and teach forever (or at least until I decide to retire, buy a farm and raise pygmy goats (not kidding, actually)). Read on!

Forty

"Let food be thy medicine and medicine be thy food."
–Hippocrates

Nutrition: Fueling Your Body

As with so many other things that have come to me later in life, I never truly understood the concept of diet as fuel for the body until I opened dance 101 in 2004. Sure, I was aware of the four major food groups and was careful to have each represented on my plate at every meal. I always kept my portions small, being careful not to overeat. But, having grown up in a Cuban family where, as my grandfather used to say, "It's not a meal unless there's dessert", I developed quite a sweet tooth. Dessert and all, I thought my diet was fine until my activity level shot up. When I opened dance 101 in 2004, I was teaching seventeen dance classes a week. This was a challenging period for me; I'd often feel tired and sluggish with a low level of energy. At the time, I chalked it up to the insane number of classes I was putting my 46 year-old body through. Jokingly I refer to this chapter in my life as "Two Advil and a Red Bull" because that's how I got through it.

But Advil and Red Bull can only band aid a situation for so long. After several months, when my body should have ramped up to meet these new physical demands, I began to think there was something else that wasn't working for me and that it might be my diet.

As I recall my former eating habits, with what I now know, I shake my head in disbelief. How could I not have made the connection between diet and proper fuel? How could I not have understood that the body responds to what we put into it? And how could I not have realized those extra twenty pounds that I carried into midlife were the result of my diet and not my metabolism slowing down due to age! Around the time I was in my mid-thirties, I was diagnosed with IBS (Irritable Bowel Syndrome) which was believed to be caused by stress. I suffered through the first years of dance 101 believing my sluggish energy level, digestive issues and extra weight were all caused by over exercising, stress and a slower metabolism. I blamed everything except what I was putting into my mouth—which over time revealed itself to be the culprit.

> **"The point I am trying to make is that no manner of exercise, no matter how frequently you do it, can compensate for a poor diet.**

I made an appointment with a nutritionist. She asked me to keep a food diary for two weeks. In the diary I had to list what I ate, how much and at what time of day. Next to each food entry I described how I felt thirty minutes later. What I anticipated to be a consultation in which I was handed a diet to follow, quickly became an investigation into which foods triggered unpleasant responses in me.

Keeping the food diary caused me to pay attention to how my body was responding to different foods. So much for my ignorance about how food affected me! Here was proof—in my own handwriting and it wasn't rocket science. I was eating foods my body couldn't process. Lactose and sugar were the primary offenders, followed by gluten. Out went dairy, sugar and bread from my diet and I began to feel better, my energy level spiked and I dropped some weight (not the full 20 lb, but maybe half of it). This was great! Well, actually it was good enough and I stopped there. My IBS continued to occasionally rear its ugly head—albeit less frequently, but still. I remained on my medication and accepted the IBS must truly be stress related. However, over the next decade, I eventually became a vegan and my IBS completely disappeared.

The point I am trying to make is that no manner of exercise, no matter how frequently you do it, can compensate for a poor diet. People who think professional athletes can eat whatever they want are mistaken. If anything, I've never met a more disciplined group of folks than those who make their living by way of their bodies. Gone are the days of a sliced turkey, Swiss cheese, mayo and lettuce sandwich for lunch. Hello, mixed greens, garbanzos, avocado, and broccoli tossed in an olive oil vinaigrette with a side of organic peanut butter. Talk about a lifestyle change! There is no eating on the run when you're a professional athlete. You have to plan and prepare your meals to make sure your body is getting the fuel and the nutrition it needs. What you choose to eat is absolutely going to impact the performance of your body.

I've never been the "my body is my temple" type (although I strive to be), but the reality of deriving a living from the use of my body motivated me to take a serious look at my eating habits. Years ago, in conversation with a fellow dance teacher about my lack of energy, I was asked (and I quote) what was I putting into my tank? He went on to ask me how far would my car go if I put rocks in the tank instead of gas? The point was that the body needs a specific kind of fuel to make it run—just like a car. Too little and you run out of gas. Use the wrong kind of gas, the car won't start. A full tank will take you 350 miles. So, what are you going to put into your tank?

The information contained in the next paragraphs is based on my own experience, years of extended research and trial and error. I am not a nutritionist nor am I a medical doctor. I share this information with you in hopes it will spark your own research to determine what works best for you. Consult with a licensed nutritionist or your doctor before making any drastic changes to your diet!

Our bodies have certain needs that must be met in order to fuel our exercise level. The body consumes calories which are then converted into energy we can use. Carbohydrates, proteins and fats are the three macromolecules that provide calories. Good carbohydrates (whole grains), legumes (chickpeas, black-eyed peas, lentils, split peas, kidney, navy, pinto beans), fruits and vegetables and healthy fats (olive oil, avocado, flaxseeds, hemp seeds, nuts) are the foundation of my diet. Carbohydrates provide about half of my energy needs while engaging in intense exercise, producing a higher level of oxygen per unit than fat, another primary source of fuel. Carbohydrates make up about 50 percent of my total calorie intake. By eating them early in the day, I fuel myself for the coming workload and by replenishing them after exercise I can keep myself consistently fueled for the remainder of the day. This is especially important when I teach multiple classes per

> **There is no eating on the run when you're a professional athlete. You have to plan and prepare your meals to make sure your body is getting the fuel and the nutrition it needs.**

day. I avoid slow digesting carbohydrates such as: soy milk, bread, rice and sugar before exercise as they can weigh the stomach and may cause heaviness and nausea. Milk and cheese are also slow digesting carbohydrates. You may not think of dairy products as carbs, but they supply lactose which is a natural sugar.

A word on "bad" carbohydrates (also known as refined carbohydrates): I avoid these as much as possible! These include sugar and processed "white" grains. A few examples are white bread, white rice and some pastas. These carbs are high in calories with little nutritional value. A sugary snack before class may give me a spike in energy, but an hour later I will crash!

Protein helps me largely with the recovery phase after class. It is the building blocks of the body, used to make muscles, tendons, organs and skin. Proteins are made of amino acids which are found in meat, fish, eggs and dairy. However, beans, nuts, seeds, grains, soy and some greens are also good sources of protein. In my research, I found that the body needs about .38 grams of protein per pound of bodyweight (this puts me at 49 grams daily, do the math to determine your own daily requirement). This should represent about 10–15 percent of my daily caloric intake. A gram of protein contains four calories. Keeping a tally of my daily intake of protein helps me ensure I am getting a sufficient amount. It is easier for me to count grams of protein than to convert the grams to calories, and this may work for you as well. Food labels always state protein content in grams.

Further, I learned that fat is the first macromolecule utilized by the body for energy and is the primary fuel source for low-level to moderate exercise such as walking or jogging and other longer endurance events that are at lower intensities. Fat consumption should be around 20–35 percent of my daily caloric intake. There are nine calories in a gram of fat. If my daily calorie intake is 2500, then I should be eating 55 to 97 grams of fat a day. A great source of healthy fat (Omega-3's) is found in fish and flaxseed.

And then there's water . . . The National Academy of Medicine recommends women consume 11 cups of water a day (88 ounces) and for men it's 15 cups (120 ounces). That's A LOT of water! At first I struggled to drink all this water until I realized I wasn't taking into account that there is water in the foods I was eating as well. Even wine is 86 percent water! Rather than religiously documenting every ounce of my fluid intake, as long as I drink water with my meals, drink a 16 oz bottle of water after each class and drink water (not sodas or juices) when I feel thirsty, I should be able to get the water I need.

My daily water ritual is one glass in the morning before my coffee, one glass with each meal, two glasses (16 oz) after class, and a glass at around 8 p.m. This provides me with about 46 ounces of additional water a day.

When I began educating myself about nutrition, I found it quite challenging to incorporate my newly acquired knowledge into practical everyday food choices. I had to develop a new habit of paying attention to labels and planning my meals. I stopped eating out for lunch as a daily routine. When I leave my house for the studio, I pack not only my lunch (carbs and fat) but also my "recovery" snack for after class (which is high in protein). I begin my day with a shake that contains all three (carbohydrates, protein and fat) which sends me into my first class well fueled. This may not be the best system for you, but after trying different approaches this one works great for me.

When you become a professional athlete, trying to lose weight while also fueling the body for exercise can be very successful as long as it's done correctly. To lose weight you must consume fewer calories than you are currently averaging, but not at the expense of healthy body function and repair. Your exercise level will already burn more calories than before, so the key is to consume enough to meet your energy levels without adding excess calories. The best way to do this is to cut out empty calories that do nothing for you (other than give you pleasure), like eating sugar and refined carbs (that the body converts into sugar).

To lose weight or to maintain the weight you currently carry, you may want to take a look at your Basal Metabolic Rate (BMR) which is the number of calories required to keep the body functioning at rest. There are a number of different formulas to calculate this (you can find them online) that factor in our gender, height, weight, and age. A more accurate model for athletes uses lean body mass (LBM) which accounts for the percentage of body fat. If you want to try this and don't know your body fat percentage, try using the former model, then add the number of calories you likely require for your total daily energy expenditure (TDEE).

To calculate the BMR for a female, I used this formula: Multiply 9.99 x weight + 6.25 x height – 4.92 x age in years – 161.

This formula is based on weight in kilograms, height in centimeters, age in years. To convert pounds to kilos, divide your weight by 2.205 and to calculate height, figure it out in inches and then multiply by 2.54. Using this formula, my BMR is 1167. This is how many calories my body needs to support vital body functions without getting out of bed.

To calculate your TDEE (Total Daily Energy Expenditure), multiply your BMR according to this chart:

Moderately Active	= BMR x 1.55
Very Active	= BMR x 1.725
Extra Active	= BMR x 1.9

Accounting for my TDEE, my body requires about 1925 calories a day to support my body function and fuel my activity. To maintain my current weight I would need to limit my daily calories to this number.

However, if I wanted to drop weight without sacrificing healthy bodily function or losing muscle mass and adequately fuel my activity level, I would need to reduce this number. As a general rule, an athlete can take in 300–500 fewer calories a day without penalty. This would result in about a one pound weight loss per week. That may not seem like a lot, but it adds up quickly. And it's safe. The worst thing, in my opinion, is to go on a crash diet. One may quickly lose more weight, but the price paid is too high. The risk of feeling miserable because the body does not have enough energy will compromise not only one's health but the enjoyment of teaching classes. Additionally, the changes you make to your diet must be relatively permanent otherwise the weight comes back on when you revert to your old habits. Once you hit your target weight, recalculate your BMR and TDEE to determine your caloric intake corresponding to your new weight and then stick to it.

If counting calories has elicited a big ::sigh:: from you, try counting grams. The most important markers, in my opinion are: sodium, sugar, fat, carbs and protein.

Here are some daily guidelines for women:

Sodium:	<1500 mg
Sugar:	<25 grams
Fat:	44-78 grams
Carbs:	225-325 grams
Protein:	>46 grams

For healthy weight loss, the most important markers for me (from the five listed above) were sodium (to avoid water retention) and sugar (to avoid adding body fat). Our bodies need carbs, fat and protein and as long as we are eating whole foods and not refined or processed foods, we can eat larger amounts of these and still lose weight. Focus on your sugar and salt intake. We know that the body converts sugar into fat. We also know that the body burns fat as its first source of fuel. So, naturally if you limit your sugar intake, the body is likely to turn to it's fuel storage for energy. Note: this may explain why people lose weight quickly when they begin exercising only to experience a slowing down of weight loss as they become leaner. Salt, the other great offender, is also worth watching. Excess salt intake causes water retention and puffiness. Increasing your water intake while decreasing your sodium intake alone may produce weight loss. Lay off those potato chips! They're lethal!

When it comes to designing and planning a beneficial and healthy diet for athletic performance and maybe weight loss, you can either follow a published diet, consult with a nutritionist for a customized diet plan, or you can educate yourself about what your body needs, then formulate your own plan. Hopefully the information I've shared with you in this chapter helps you take a step in the right direction. Whatever you decide, please strongly consider the importance of a healthy diet in your new profession as a teacher!

Forty-one

"If you listen to your body when it whispers,
you will never have to listen to it scream."
–Old Adage

Recovery, Injury Prevention and Care

W hen we engage in a physical occupation, we quickly realize how sensitive our body is to our lifestyle. This heightened level of awareness comes to us because we depend on the performance of our bodies to earn our livelihood. A minor injury here and there and occasional muscle soreness is a fact of life for those of us in this profession. How we react to the messages our bodies send us will dictate how long we will be able to continue doing what we are doing. If we ignore the signs, we pay the consequences. Pay attention, and reap the benefits.

Learning to "listen to your body" will most likely prolong your career, keeping you active for the long run. Our bodies are constantly communicating with us, whether it's an upset stomach after something we eat, or a stress headache or any number of minor ailments that can send us to bed for a few days. Our bodies are programmed for survival, and when we are over exerting ourselves, the body may knock us back and make us rest. When we engage in a new physical activity, or increase the frequency of an existing activity, the body can tense up in self-defense and if we ignore the warning signs and push through it, we may likely injure ourselves.

{ **Our body is constantly communicating with us—and it expects us to listen. When we don't, the message gets louder.** }

The year was 1999 and it was my third stage performance. I was dancing in a complex piece that had eleven formational changes. The piece was five minutes long. All in all, I had to learn around 625 counts of choreography and perform these steps at a pretty fast clip. We rehearsed for about a month, several times per week, with each rehearsal lasting about two hours. Before long, I started chugging energy drinks during these rehearsals to help me physically get through them. Had I known then what I know now, my constant need for an energy boost would have tipped me off that I was on the verge of an injury (as injuries are prone to happen when the body is experiencing fatigue).

One week before opening night, while doing some light housework at home, I bent over to pick something up and felt a really terrible shooting pain in my lower back. I couldn't straighten back up. Off to the chiropractor I went and after several very unpleasant adjustments, I was told to rest. There went the performance I had rehearsed so diligently for the past month. I was heartbroken and I sulked. Then suddenly out of the blue, my back pain left me (just as instantly as it had appeared) and I literally got out of bed, got dressed and headed over to the studio for rehearsal.

Come opening night I had pretty much forgotten about this little incident. Excited for the performance, adrenaline racing through me, I stepped onto the stage and the piece began. Not one minute into the performance, on stage, I did a simple pivot turn and my left knee dislocated, snapping my ACL. I dove into the wings, clutching my knee in excruciating pain. A fellow dancer backstage wrapped up my knee and found some ice to put on it. Fortunately my knee popped back into place and I was able to hobble to my car and drive myself home. I cried a river on that drive home. I knew I had done something serious.

Injuries and body aches are to be expected. No professional athlete can escape this reality. However, a small injury or discomfort can be the precursor to a bigger one and if we are not paying attention, our body will definitively have the last word. Some minor injuries are just that and if we immediately respond, the likelihood of another bigger injury may be avoided. But here's the thing: if we are earning our living from our classes, a missed class can translate into a cut in pay and this is where the practicality of resting can be perceived as a luxury.

Teaching while injured is an eventuality you will most likely face. Before you cringe, let me assure you it is a lot easier than you might expect. In fact, teaching movement without the benefit of using your body to demonstrate is an opportunity to deepen your teaching skills. Removing your body from the equation may take something away—but in doing so; it can add a new element by heightening other aspects of your teaching. If you ask a student to demonstrate, this greatly contributes to that student. It's flattering and encouraging when a teacher asks his/her student to demonstrate. This will also cause you to be more hands on with your other students—which everyone appreciates. Your students care about you. If you are healing an injury, they will rally around you. Don't hesitate to ask for help or to show up vulnerable. People love to help out. Don't deny your students the opportunity to express how much they care for you! They want you to heal!

If you suffer an injury that lands you in bed, you must go there. If your body is in pain, you must not put any stress on it. If you are sick, coughing, and have a fever, you should not be teaching. Hopefully you have insurance (because it is a necessity in this profession) and some savings to help you through. Prepare in advance for the eventuality something like this might happen! If you set aside 10 percent of your earnings every month, in ten

> " **Teaching while injured is an eventuality you will most likely face. Before you cringe, let me assure you it is a lot easier than you might expect.**

months you will have one month's salary on hand. In the words of John F. Kennedy: *"The best time to repair the roof is when the sun is shining."* You are going into a physical occupation. Your body is not a machine, and even if it were, machines break down. Be prepared!

As a matter of everyday practice, there are things you can do to lessen the likelihood of injury or speed up your recovery from them. With a little bit of awareness and a heavy dose of respect for your body, here are a few daily habits you can engage in that will ward off injury— especially if you are teaching a large number of classes.

Rest and Recovery

Athletes must rest their bodies. What constitutes a good night's sleep varies among individuals. Some people may only require six hours or less, and some need a full eight to nine. Once you determine how many hours your body needs, you must make sure to get that amount of sleep on the evenings before you teach. Additionally, if you teach multiple classes per day, don't be surprised if you also need a thirty-minute nap midway through. Rest is critically important because this is when the body recharges and heals itself. Fatigue invites injury and lack of sleep prolongs recovery. Take a close look at your sleeping habits. I strongly advise you make sure you are getting enough sleep!

Pacing and Rhythm

Try to schedule classes with sufficient recovery time in-between. Avoid teaching back to back high intensity classes as a regular habit (every once in a while won't hurt). Ideally, alternate intensity when possible. Three classes a day is not uncommon for a full-time teacher. More than three can lead to burnout in a few months, if you are actually "doing" your classes along with your students. This is where it comes in handy to teach multiple disciplines or variations of the same thing. If you are teaching three classes a day, ideally you'll be teaching one low, mid, and high impact class. Teaching three high impact classes a day on your regular schedule will wear you out faster than you can imagine. Even if your diet and water intake are on point, this level of physical and mental output is extremely hard on the body. Pace yourself wisely!

Watch for Warning Signs

Make the practice of listening to your body a daily ritual, especially on the days you teach.

When you get home at the end of your work day, take a nice HOT shower. The heat on your body stimulates your circulation sending nourishing blood to every muscle, tendon and ligament. Moist heat is very healing. Hot tub baths with Epsom salts work miracles. If you go to bed relaxed, your body should rest well (as long as your mind chatter doesn't keep you up!).

Muscle soreness typically shows up in the mornings. Give yourself extra time in the shower with the hot water running over whichever part of you is sore. If the soreness is bothersome, you can sometimes take an anti-inflammatory (but not as a regular habit). If it's a teaching day, you must take it easy. Try to avoid working your sore muscles. Prevailing wisdom is that it takes one to two days for soreness to go away. You may still be able to teach class, just sit out any movement that involves those specific muscles until they heal.

> **Make the practice of listening to your body a daily ritual, especially on the days you teach.**

Injury requires immediate icing. You can ice for forty-eight hours where you are experiencing some swelling. According to my physician, ice packs reduce bleeding into the tissues, and can reduce muscle spasms and pain. His advice to me is to ice for fifteen minutes at a time, rest for fifteen, then repeat, and never directly on the skin (to avoid ice burns). Also important is to elevate the injured area above the heart. This helps to avoid gravity pooling liquid around the injury. The golden rule for muscle injury is the RICE method: Rest, Ice, Compression, Elevation. However, if pain persists and/or symptoms do not resolve within several days, see your doctor.

I've also learned not to apply heat to an injury that is swollen because heat simply draws more blood to the area and worsens the swelling.

My general rule is: soreness = heat. Injury = ice and elevation. Heat draws blood, cold dispels it.

Additionally, a compression wrap works very well for the reduction of swelling and helps to stabilize an injured joint. However, wrapping the injury does not mean you are free to stress the joint. You must allow the joint to heal because if it does not heal correctly, it could become unstable, weak and possibly re-injured. Try to immobilize the joint as much as possible until you are able to receive medical care.

Avoid Activities which May Injure You

There are a number of physical activities I enjoy. I grew up horseback riding and I love to ride. I enjoy playing kickball and tennis. While I may occasionally indulge these pleasures, for the most part, I do so very cautiously. Any activity my body is not used to doing represents a risk to me. It's a matter of priorities. I love to teach my classes. My ability to teach is very important to me. I am extremely protective of my body. Infrequent or new activities can be risky for me. I know that if I do what my body is accustomed to doing, the likelihood of an injury is greatly reduced. I don't mean to suggest you stop doing any physical activity you enjoy—just be careful. Remember what is at stake

What I Pack in My Work Bag

My teacher bag always includes a few staple items:

- An ace bandage
- A knee and ankle brace
- A bag of "instant" cold
- An anti-inflammatory

This is my first aid kit. I know these items will help me stabilize most minor injuries, reducing swelling and pain. This is my first line of defense until I get home or to an urgent care center (depending on the severity of the injury). Plan a first aid kit that best suits you and your personal needs. You may ask your doctor for advice as well. Being well prepared can help immensely when needed!

Plan for Regular Body Maintenance

Chiropractic adjustments can be hugely beneficial to some teachers. It is estimated that 90 percent of all world class athletes use chiropractic care to help prevent injuries and increase performance.

Chiropractic aligns the body. One of the biggest causes of injuries in athletes is asymmetry throughout the body, meaning one side of the body is different than the other. This means one side of the body has to over compensate for the other side, making it susceptible to strain. Chiropractic will balance the body by addressing these asymmetries. Regular chiropractic adjustments will increase range of motion in your joints and promote faster healing. I personally have benefited greatly from chiropractic care.

Massage Therapy

Research shows that in relation to exercise and athletic performance, massage can reduce muscle tension, promote relaxation, increase range of motion, decrease muscle stiffness and soreness, enhance athletic performance and help prevent injuries. Many teachers I work with get regular massages—varying in frequency. It is a budgetary and personal preference as to how often, but these teachers regard their massages as a necessity, not a luxury. Many say that the benefits are certainly worth it. If massage resonates with you, you may want to consult your doctor before taking the time to find the right massage therapist for you and your activity level. It could be very beneficial to your overall well-being.

With time you will know exactly what your body needs, you will learn to listen to your body, what resonates with you, and you will develop an inner compass that will guide your activity level. Take good care of your body! Be mindful of what you put into it and be respectful of its need for rest and recovery. Your body is your temple . . . and now it's also your profession.

Forty-two

"Rest and self-care are so important. When you take time to replenish your spirit, it allows you to serve others from the overflow. You cannot serve from an empty vessel."
–Eleanor Brownn

Mind Energy Conspirators and How to Deal with Them

*M*ind energy is the energy of our thoughts. What we think and the thoughts we choose to repeat are the architects of our life. Our thoughts create our reality. They determine how we perceive and respond to what is happening around us. Our thoughts can be exhausting and mind energy can become depleted, interfering with our ability to give. Conversely, they can be uplifting and motivating, adding great enthusiasm to what we give. Either way, as a teacher coming into contact with many people, how well we manage and recharge our thoughts is directly related to the class experience we create for others. This includes our ability to protect ourselves from the disabling consequences of runaway emotions and in the times where we cannot shield ourselves, to bounce back from them. I touch on this throughout this book, especially in Part 1, but I'd like to revisit the subject here from a different perspective: one of self-care.

Neutralizing our emotions in order to approach our classes from a clean slate requires a certain degree of mind energy all by itself. But when we layer-in additional environmental stressors, it can become overwhelming. This chapter addresses several scenarios of environmental conditions which deplete mind energy (and can interfere with your ability to neutralize), along with suggestions on how to manage, cope or overcome these additional burdens. I guess you could call this "the mental health chapter". I want you to take care of yourself! Mind, body and spirit!

There are a few things that can be done to replenish mind energy and as a teacher, you should be aware of what they are so you can recharge for the next day or your next class. You should also be aware of which kinds of scenarios are likely to deplete you more than others so you can anticipate them.

 Mental exhaustion is just as intrusive as physical exhaustion and in a class setting, a teacher is burning energy on both these levels.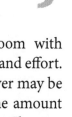

Extraordinary teachers are givers. Filling a room with nurturing energy demands a conscious level of intention and effort. It requires us to become neutral in order to give. Whatever may be going on in our lives at any moment will determine the amount of energy needed to reach that inner state of neutrality. Clearing ourselves of grief, inner torment, frustration or anger can deplete us before we even walk into the class. And even if we are not going through a challenging period in our personal lives, the simple act of teaching several classes in one day can deplete us as the day goes on. Mind energy depletion will wear us down. It can seep into our classes and tag others. And if we don't recover the spent energy, it may become a chronic condition that can compound into a devastating quagmire. As a teacher, you must take care of your mind and spirit to the same degree you nourish and care for your body. If you are new to teaching, you may not have any idea where to begin or how to care for your mind. The following is what I've been able to identify based upon my own personal experiences. As with the bulk of what you've read in this book so far, the only reason I can describe these scenarios to you is because I am no stranger to them.

I call them "Mind Energy Conspirators" because oftentimes these triggers are not singular: rather they typically overlap, "conspiring" among themselves, joining forces and working together to wreak havoc on our mind health!

Some of these conspirators are:

- Ongoing personal trauma (what is happening in your personal life in a particular moment)
- Illness
- Fatigue
- Lack of sleep, rest and recovery
- A bad day
- Over-stimulation

Personal Trauma

After opening dance 101 in 2004, my life fell apart. During the first few years after launching the studio when the business was at its most vulnerable, demanding I work fourteen hour days and teach seventeen classes a week, my husband asked me for a divorce. In the following year, my mother died suddenly of a heart attack while I was teaching class, followed by my brother eight months later who died of a drug overdose at 51. I felt my world falling apart and the burden of my grief weighed so heavily on me, I often felt I couldn't face the day—much less the classes

> " **As unbelievable as it may sound, acceptance is the only thing I have found that can neutralize the impact of trauma.**

I had to teach. I could have closed the studio and remained in bed all day but that would have added yet another great loss to my growing list. I had to pull myself up by my boot straps, shower, put on my make-up and face the day . . . and my students.

Throughout this book I have repeatedly mentioned purpose, acceptance and gratitude. These values are of great importance to me because it was my willingness to embrace them that enabled me to manage this devastating period in my life. I held on to these values so tightly at the time that they since have become woven into the fabric of my being and continue with me to this day. It was the remembrance of my purpose as a teacher, the acceptance of that which I cannot control, and gratitude for the path I am on that gave me a "super power" kind of determination to face this degree of adversity.

Teaching is a noble profession. What we do touches people's lives and, make no mistake, everybody, and I mean everybody, is going through something. Nobody gets a free ride in life—no matter what their lives may look like on the outside. On any given day we will have people in our class who are struggling and the hour they spend with us may be the only reprieve they'll have on that day. We can make a difference in the lives of every soul who chooses to give us his/her time. This is what I mean when I talk about purpose. Believing this to-the-letter is what helps me remain focused on the importance of my contribution to the world. Giving to others gives my life meaning. It is my purpose. My purpose matters. I matter. Life can knock me down, but I have a job to do—and so do you.

Life will throw us curve balls every so often. Things will happen to us that hit us out of nowhere and all we can do is take the hit. Complaining about it might make us feel a little better, but it won't change what's happened. As unbelievable as it may sound, acceptance is the only thing I have found that can neutralize the impact of trauma. Acceptance does not mean I agree with what has happened, nor does it make the pain of loss disappear. But it helps—even if only slightly. Acceptance means: I acknowledge that I cannot change whatever has happened—only my attitude about it. As Holocaust survivor Viktor E. Frankl so famously said:

> ❝ ***Everything can be taken from a man but one thing: the last of human freedoms—to choose one's attitude in any given set of circumstances.***

I believe gratitude is the greatest human energy force on this planet. When we express gratitude for our blessings we increase the probability they will remain or continue. Expressing gratitude when things are falling apart is not easy; however, it's during these periods when the expression of gratitude is at its most powerful because it causes a redirection of focus. I was not grateful for the loss of my marriage, my mother and my brother. But I was grateful for the time I had with them. And I was grateful for my kids, my business, my classes, my friends, the comfortable bed I sleep in, the home I live in, my good health, my safety, security and well-being, to name a few.

When personal trauma has me in its ugly grip, I express purpose, acceptance and gratitude in a louder voice during my daily contemplation (more on this later) and throughout my day—especially right before I walk into class. This helps me put things into perspective, clear myself out as much as possible and set my emotions to neutral so that I may be a conduit of good for others—if only for that hour. Maybe this strategy can work for you as well!

Illness

I have always regarded minor illness as a wake-up call from the universe that I need to stop what I am doing and recharge. I've noticed that when I catch a "bug", it typically coincides with my experiencing stress, lack of sleep and fatigue. Much has been written about how our immune system can be weakened by environmental stressors and I believe this is true. I have learned to anticipate catching something when I know I'm burning the candle on both ends. I do my best to pull back and take care of myself before the universe taps me on the shoulder. Being sick not only does a number on the body, it depletes mind energy as well. Have you ever noticed how being sick brings you emotionally "down"?

Illness delivers a double whammy: body and mind. The good news is when the body begins to feel better, the mind tends to follow suit. The important thing here is to be aware not to make any big decisions (if possible) while you're sick and if you find yourself thinking unkind thoughts, do not take them seriously (and certainly do not act upon them!). Surrender to what has you. Acknowledge it. Follow your doctor's instructions and enjoy the extra bed time. Read. Binge on movies. There's nothing you can do about it so accept it and focus your energy on getting better. Tell any negative thoughts that pop into your head to go take a hike. Make the best of your surprise "staycation". As miserable as you may feel, it's only smart to rest and allow your body to pool its energy and reserves to fight the bug that's got you.

Whatever you do, do not teach when you should be in bed! It will only delay your recovery and you might pass the bug to a student. I know this is easier said than done. You have financial obligations. However, you must trust in the benevolence of the universe to provide for you. This may sound "woo woo" radical and it is not at all easy to do—even if you believe it. Trust! We tend to think we know what's better for us than the universe. But, I'm 60 years into this life and I'm here to tell you we don't. All things happen for a reason—yada, yada, yada—but it is true. If we trust in the wisdom of the universe which is so much more expansive, older, powerful, wiser and more knowledgeable than we, we should be able to relax for a minute to allow our bodies to heal.

Fatigue and Lack of Sleep

Fatigue is the result of over-exertion. When we have over-worked ourselves, we feel tired and worn out. In this weakened state, our body pulls energy from every possible reserve to keep us going. This includes the energy it pulls from our minds. The resulting depletion of mind energy can cause us to be irritable, impatient and unreasonable not to mention, unfriendly!

Lack of sleep can affect us in varying degrees, depending on the deficiency we are experiencing. A few hours less of sleep may go unnoticed, but increase or double that amount and the mind energy kicks in to make up for the difference. Lack of sleep may also cause fatigue, so if we combine the two, we've got a powder keg of a day to get through!

Prevention is really the only way to successfully manage fatigue. But once we find ourselves in the throes of it, the best course of action is to push through as best we can and head for home as soon as possible. Drink as much water as we can and crash on the couch or go directly to bed. This will give us the necessary recovery. Only rest and limited stimulation can "cure" fatigue that is caused by over-exertion.

As a professional athlete, you must be able to identify the needs of your mind and body in order to achieve an optimal output. This is not something you should ignore. It may take some trial and error, unfortunately, but the benefits of identifying your physical and emotional limits are endless. It requires you to pay attention to how your body performs, reacts, and feels, and in this process you will learn a great deal about your physical needs and limitations. Understanding how fatigue and lack of sleep affect your mind energy empowers you to prevent it from happening whenever possible.

To determine your threshold of physical output (that may lead to fatigue), my suggestion is that you give thoughtful consideration to the five markers I've identified below. You can begin with an estimate, and tweak it over time.

1. What is the minimum amount of sleep you need to feel rested? _____

2. Based on how you feel at the end of a day in which you have taught multiple classes, how many do you think you can realistically teach in one day without your body or mind feeling sluggish? _____

3. Given the compounding effect of teaching multiple classes, how many can you teach over a seven day period? (You may not know yet how many classes you are capable of teaching, just make a guess.) _____

4. How many non-teaching hours can you work in one day without becoming overwhelmed? _____

5. How many full days off per week do you need to feel recharged? _____

Now take a look at the values you've identified. Hours of sleep and full days off constitute a minimum number you require. The number of classes and hours worked is a maximum number. Hold steadfast to these numbers once you've tweaked them for accuracy. Any deviation from these numbers may spell trouble for you and since we are talking about mind energy conspirators, the consequences of violating these numbers will spill over into other areas and compound into a more stressful situation to manage.

A Bad Day

Philosophically speaking, bad days are necessary. Without them, good days would pass by unnoticed. Having a point of reference enables us to identify and label what we consider to be good. We need our bad days! However, when they appear, bad days can do a number on our minds. Anger, frustration, sadness, worry and aggravation gobble up mind energy. These are "needy" emotions that want to take hostage every thought we think. And as skilled as we may become at "clearing" ourselves out to teach class, as soon as class is over, here come those rabble-rousers running back in to eat up our mind energy once again. Pesky little fellas!

The best remedy for a bad day (in my opinion) is to do something nice for yourself. For me, that something can be as simple as picking up an almond croissant on my drive home. They are my favorite! Or a nice long hot shower or tub bath. Maybe I'll turn off my phone and pick up a book or watch a funny movie on TV. Life is full of tiny pleasures, and it can be anything—as long as it brings a smile to your face. You'd be surprised at how little it takes to turn a bad day around when you put a conscious effort into it—if it's one day. If you're going through a series of bad days, then that's a period and a completely different ballgame (reference personal trauma a few pages back).

Overstimulation

The first time I said: "We are located next to the Liquid Lumberdators" I didn't even notice. "Do you mean the Lumber Liquidators?" someone asked. The second time I said it, I laughed. By the third time, I knew. I was depleted. If you've ever worked a trade show, you may be able to relate. That day, on my feet for hours on end while answering what seemed to be a million questions about the concept of my studio, I was about to keel over—barely six hours in. We begin each day with a specific amount of energy to give and if we hit empty, there's no more to pull from. My enthusiastic descriptions of the studio had redacted from a lengthy monologue to "Like to dance? Come see us! Next!" Haha! To this day, when I find my mind energy has been depleted to the point where I cannot speak another word to anyone, I say I've been "liquid lumberdated" and my family knows not to speak to me.

There is only one remedy for complete mind energy depletion: silence. If and when you find yourself in this state: retreat!

Certain circumstances are ripe for overstimulation. A great example is teaching to a large class (twenty or more) of students unknown to you. If you are connected to this number of people you are receiving an enormous amount of information in every second that passes. It takes quite a bit of mind energy to receive and process this amount of information continuously for an hour. However, if you know the majority of the students in the class—to the degree that you know them by name and know about their class history and their level of ability, you won't be as over stimulated.

Any situation, in which you must interact, connect with or speak to a large number of people during a specified period of time, may be over stimulating. There really isn't much you can do to avoid this, but you can recover quickly. All you need is some peace and quiet.

Apart from the scenarios above, we burn up mind energy

everyday by simply living our lives. Developing a strategy to replenish ourselves is truly a personal and individual journey. Knowing that a strategy is needed is 90 percent of having one developed. Give some thought to your personal needs and develop your own personal routine to recharge.

Here are Some Additional Suggestions for You

Contemplate (or meditate). Set aside ten minutes out of your day to sit quietly and watch your thoughts fly past. Set your alarm ten minutes earlier and make this a part of your morning ritual. I do not recommend you do this in the evening. Your mind energy may be depleted or you may be consumed by something that happened earlier in the day. Ruminating on these thoughts late at night may interfere with your ability to fall asleep. The mind declutters itself while we sleep. Mornings, in my opinion, are much better for contemplation.

If something is weighing on your mind, distract yourself before bedtime. Watch a movie or read a book in bed until you fall asleep. Worrisome thoughts have a tendency to go around and around and around in our minds, requiring a "break state" to interrupt the cycle. I don't think it is possible to think away our thoughts—if you know what I mean. Our mind's capacity to latch tightly onto thoughts is quite impressive and worse, it gets used to thinking the same thoughts and delights in thinking them ad nauseam.

Don't let negative thoughts become a pattern of your thinking. As my former teacher, Jerry Stocking once said to me: *"Any thought we think twice defines us."* I don't necessarily agree with it requiring only two times but I do believe there is a number. Maybe ten times? Twenty? One Hundred? Two? Whatever that number is, be mindful of what you repeatedly think. I catch myself when I say or think things I really would prefer the universe not to hear, like "I'm too old for this!" "I am so tired and over it!" "I want to live on an island away from people!" The list goes on.

> **And, when you want something,
> all the universe conspires in helping
> you to achieve it.**
> **–Paulo Coelho, The Alchemist**

Honestly, I don't want to live on a island, be too old for anything or be so frustrated with life that I want to check out. If it is true that the universe conspires (and I do believe this), I don't want it to hear me complain about anything—because it might bring more of that particular thing into my life! The universe holds no value judgments. It does not distinguish between right and wrong, good or bad. What it repeatedly hears, it conspires to bring into being. That's a sobering thought, isn't it?

Write Your "Morning Pages"

I was first introduced to this concept by Julia Cameron in her celebrated book: *The Artist's Way: A Spiritual Path to Higher Creativity (Penguin Putnam Inc, 2002)*. Specifically, this is an exercise in which you handwrite stream of consciousness onto a sheet of paper that you throw away. She calls this practice the "Morning Pages" which act as a mind dump to get rid of the clutter in your brain. What is written is not meant to be read nor kept. No need to proofread or correct spelling . . . it's trash! You are simply downloading thoughts onto paper in order to free-up mind space for new, other thoughts (hopefully positive ones!) to enter. When I would write my morning pages, I would close my eyes as I wrote and visualize the words leaving my mind, traveling down my arm to my hand to the pen and onto the paper. I don't remember writing a single cohesive paragraph. But boy, was it powerful! I remember realizing how many useless thoughts I had knocking about in my head and once I purged them, my mind felt "lighter". Try this! See what it clears up for you!

What's important here is that you factor in an appropriate amount of balance into your life. I cannot stress enough how necessary this is. Teaching can be an exhilarating vocation ripe with tremendous rewards, but it can be depleting at times. Whether you balance out your work with a hobby, other interests or plenty of down time, it is critical for you to recharge your physical and mind energy on a regular basis. You cannot give from an empty well. Replenish!

Be protective of your time and your needs. Avoid pushing yourself too hard. This can be a real challenge because the more exceptional you are at teaching, the more invitations and opportunities will appear for you. Not every request should be met with an enthusiastic "yes!" Once you've hit your maximum class load, respect that number. If a fantastic opportunity presents itself, replace a class instead of adding one more.

I must admit that when my body was younger I was much less respectful of it. I took for granted that it would always perform for me and when I was tired and burnt out, I'd just reach for an energy drink and push through it. But over time and a few unpleasant experiences under my belt, I've learned to care for myself with great respect and reverence.

Take care of your body, your mind and your soul. Nurture yourself so you can nurture others. At the end of the day, this is a life well lived and worth celebrating—in every regard.

ABOUT THE AUTHOR

Ofelia is the creator and director of one of the most celebrated and prominent dance studios in the United States: dance 101. Singularly the largest adult only dance studio of its kind, dance 101, was recognized by Billboard Magazine (March 2017) as one of the top ten dance studios in the country. With five studios and two locations offering over 160 weekly classes and employing 53 of Atlanta's most talented dance teachers and choreographers, dance 101 changed the landscape of dance in 2004 with its (never thought possible) combination of what historically had been two mutually exclusive industries: professional (technical) dance and dance fitness. Ofelia's approach to teaching movement to adults has enabled dance 101 to successfully develop adult beginner dancers into formidable and even world class dancers. Her teaching methods and her ability to recognize, hire and train extraordinary teachers has grown dance 101 from its original 35 students in 2004 to over 40,000 registered dancers in 2017, and growing.

Ofelia's story has been featured in numerous magazine articles (both national and local), television spots, webisodes, radio interviews, podcasts and recently in CNN Success Stories, Passion to Portfolio, Making It in America (both CNN domestic and International) as well as CNN Headline and local news broadcasts. In July, 2011 Ofelia was invited by the White House to deliver the key note speech at the Atlanta Urban Entrepreneurship Forum and was presented with The Phoenix Award by Mayor Kasim Reed. She was featured in the top 10 Atlanta Best Self magazine's Over 40 and Fabulous Atlantans and was one of 50 women profiled in Marlo Thomas's book, *It Ain't Over... Till It's Over. (Simon & Schuster, Inc. 2014)*

Ofelia's career and self-proclaimed life purpose "to bring dance into the lives of as many people as possible" has launched her into the public eye both locally and nationally as she, along with her daughter Paulina de La Valette and son Erik Soderstrom work daily to improve people's lives through dance, one step at a time.

BIBLIOGRAPHY

Cameron, Julia. The Artist's Way: A Spiritual Path to Higher Creativity. New York: Penguin Putnam Inc., 2002.

Collins, Jim. Good to Great: Why Some Companies Make the Leap . . . and Others Don't.
New York: HarperCollins Publisher, Inc., 2001.

Covey, Stephen R. The 7 Habits of Highly Effective People: Powerful Lessons in Personal Change. New York: Fireside, Simon & Schuster Inc., 1990.

Duhigg, Charles. The Power of Habit: Why We Do What We Do in Life and Business.
New York: Random House Trade Paperback, 2014.

Fowler, James H. (2008, December 5) Dynamic spread of happiness in a large social network: longitudinal analysis over 20 years in the Framingham Heart Study. Retrieved from http://www.bmj.com/content/337/bmj.a2338

Frankl, Viktor E. Man's Search for Meaning. Boston, Massachusetts: Beacon Press, 2006.
Goddard, Neville. The Power of Awareness. Pacific Publishing Studio. 2010.
Kelly, Jason. Sweat Equity: Inside the New Economy of Mind and Body. Hoboken, New Jersey: John Wiley & Sons, Inc., 2016.

Moore, John D., Dr. (2015, March 15). Gratitude and Karma. Retrieved from http://www.mychicagotherapist.com/5-ways-gratitude-attracts-positive-karma/

Nagrin, Daniel. How to Dance Forever: Surviving Against the Odds. New York: HarperCollins Publisher, Inc., 1988.

Peck, Scott. The Road Less Traveled: A New Psychology of Love, Traditional Values and Spiritual Growth. New York: Touchstone, Simon & Schuster, 2003.

Reiman, Joey. The Story of Purpose: The Path to Creating a Brighter Brand, a Greater company, and a Lasting Legacy. Hoboken, New Jersey: John Wiley & Sons, Inc., 2013.

Ruiz, Don Miguel. The Four Agreements: A Personal Guide to Personal Freedom. (A Toltec Wisdom Book). San Rafael, California: Amber-Allen Publishing, Inc., 2001.

Ruiz, Don Miguel. The Mastery of Love: A Practical Guide to the Art of Relationship (A Toltec Wisdom Book). San Rafael, California: Amber-Allen Publishing, Inc., 1999.

Simon, Sinek with David Mead and Peter Docker. Find Your Why: A Practical Guide for Discovering Purpose For You and Your Team. New York: Penguin Random House LLC, 2017.

Singer, Michael A. The Untethered Soul: The Journey Beyond Yourself. Oakland, Canada: New Harbinger Publications, Inc., 2007.

Skinner B.F. Beyond Freedom & Dignity. Harmondsworth, Middlesex, England: Penguin Books Ltd, 1971.

Tharpe, Twyla. The Creative Habit: Learn It and Use It for Life. New York: Simon & Schuster Paperbacks, 2006.

Twist, Lynne. The Soul of Money: Transforming Your Relationship with Money and Life. New York: W.W. Norton & Company, Inc., 2003.

Made in the USA
San Bernardino, CA
14 June 2020

73416840R00190